'Sustainability is a vivid and troubling term and refers to a contemporary bricolage of ideas and concepts. In this kind of muddle we need sense making and help in our sense making. We need to be clear on our language above all if we are to push back against all forms of confusion. This dictionary gathers the language and explains the terms which the sustainability community uses. In reaching out to the wider world we need to be clear. Here is help on the way.'

Simon Bell, Open University, UK

'Hello. Do you speak Sustainability? Are you fluent – or struggling to find the words? Don't fret! Margaret Robertson's dictionary decodes the lingo – at a time when this rapidly evolving agenda increasingly cross-connects with all languages (including Architecture, Business, Chemistry, Engineering and Politics) and all aspects of life, human or non-human.'

John Elkington, Volans, UK

'These days every thinking person follows a wide range of environmental issues, each issue entailing its own vocabulary. Hence the usefulness of this concise reference book. Keep it on your computer desk; you'll find yourself consulting it often – and learning an amazing number of useful terms.'

Richard Heinberg, Post Carbon Institute, USA

'Building a more sustainable world requires that we have a common understanding and language for what this means. The *Dictionary of Sustainability* is an invaluable book to help us navigate this critical journey.'

Sandra Postel, Global Water Policy Project, USA

'Words and phrases that describe an endeavor are crucial for establishing common understanding from which progressive thoughts and actions can emerge. All the more so for sustainability, a complex body of knowledge with a vast array of terms, many of which have multiple and often confusing meanings. Robertson's *Dictionary of Sustainability* is a long overdue reference work, certain to enlighten as well as provide needed uniformity.'

Thomas L. Theis, University of Illinois at Chicago, USA

'Informed conversation about sustainability requires a shared vocabulary. This noble work provides the concisely defined words and thus the concepts so vital to a progressive, desirable future.'

Tyler Volk, New York University, USA

NOV 0 7 2017

Dictionary of Sustainability

Sustainability is a diverse, interdisciplinary field focused on identifying how human culture and all living systems of the biosphere can endure and thrive into the long-term future. An extensive vocabulary has developed which draws on an increasingly large and varied range of scientific and intellectual frameworks. At the same time, a massive quantity of information of differing degrees of quality is available through the Internet, meaning that searching and sorting through details and conflicting descriptions can become a lengthy undertaking.

The *Dictionary of Sustainability* provides authoritative and accessible definitions of standard terms in use by scholars and practitioners in the emerging interdisciplinary field of sustainability. While written in lexical format, this book provides a clear and thorough conceptual framework for readers and uses language designed for clarity and comprehension in order to promote understanding and to encourage further reading. The work features careful use of cross-references, and includes several expanded entries to provide readers with nuanced understanding of important topics.

The compact size and clarity of language make this dictionary an ideal entry point for the general reader. The dictionary will also be essential reading for both undergraduate and postgraduate students studying sustainability topics.

Margaret Robertson is a member of the American Society of Landscape Architects (ASLA) and teaches at Lane Community College in Eugene, Oregon, USA where she coordinates the Sustainability degree program. She is the author of *Sustainability Principles and Practice* (Routledge, 2014).

Dictionary of Sustainability

Margaret Robertson

1390937

Routledge
Taylor & Francis Group
LONDON AND NEW YORK

earthscan
from Routledge

First published 2017
by Routledge
2 Park Square, Milton Park, Abingdon, Oxon OX14 4RN

and by Routledge
711 Third Avenue, New York, NY 10017

Routledge is an imprint of the Taylor & Francis Group, an informa business

British Library Cataloguing-in-Publication Data
A catalogue record for this book is available from the British Library

Library of Congress Cataloging-in-Publication Data
Names: Robertson, Margaret, author.
Title: Dictionary of sustainability / Margaret Robertson.
Description: First edition. | New York : Routledge, 2017.
Identifiers: LCCN 2016049337 | ISBN 9781138690820 (hbk) |
ISBN 9781138690837 (pbk) | ISBN 9781315536705 (ebk)
Subjects: LCSH: Sustainable living—Dictionaries. |
Sustainability—Dictionaries.
Classification: LCC GE196.R635 2017 | DDC 338.9/2703—dc23
LC record available at https://lccn.loc.gov/2016049337

ISBN: 978-1-138-69082-0 (hbk)
ISBN: 978-1-138-69083-7 (pbk)
ISBN: 978-1-315-53670-5 (ebk)

Typeset in Bembo
by Apex CoVantage, LLC

Printed and bound in the United States of America by
Edwards Brothers Malloy on sustainably sourced paper

Contents

Preface

Sustainability is a diverse, interdisciplinary field focused on identifying how human culture and all living systems of the biosphere can endure and thrive into the long-term future. It involves a multidimensional body of knowledge at multiple scales. As a result, an extensive vocabulary has developed which draws on an increasingly large and varied range of scientific and intellectual frameworks. At the same time, a massive quantity of information of differing degrees of quality is available through the Internet, so that searching and sorting through details and conflicting descriptions can become a lengthy undertaking.

The purpose of this dictionary is to provide the reader with the necessary vocabulary, defined authoritatively and with precision. Without a dictionary, readers must conduct their own time-consuming process of searching, finding, and evaluating masses of information. With this dictionary, the work of evaluating and distilling technical material has been done, allowing the reader quickly to find a clear and concise explanation of a term.

This dictionary gives precise definitions of terms. It is not an encyclopedia and does not include names of people, written works, or organizations (with a few essential exceptions such as the IPCC). Research and work in the field of sustainability are constantly expanding and changing, with important contributions from myriad people, sources, and organizations. To give coverage to all these elements in a single volume would be impractical. This dictionary both allows understanding and provides the solid foundation for further research by bringing authoritative clarity to each concept.

Entries are cross-referenced using these standard conventions: *Compare*, to identify a contrasting meaning; *See also*, to direct the reader to another entry where additional information can be found; and ★, an asterisk to mark a term that is defined elsewhere in its own entry.

A

ABS *See* acrylonitrile butadiene styrene.

abiotic
Nonliving. *Compare* biotic.

absorber
The dark external surface of the *thermal mass in *passive solar design.

absorptance
The property of a material in which *radiation is converted to *sensible heat; the ratio of incident radiation to radiation absorbed.

absorption
A process in which a fluid enters a porous solid material.

absorption chiller
A mechanical device which uses a heat source rather than a mechanical compressor to drive a refrigeration cycle, often as part of a *combined heat and power system.

AC *See* alternating current.

acceleration *See* Great Acceleration.

access economy *See* sharing economy.

accreditation
The process of granting credentials to an *organization based on conformance to recognized standards and attested by a third party.

ACH *See* air changes per hour.

acidic
Having a *pH below 7; a substance that donates *hydrogen ions. *Compare* alkaline.

acid mine drainage
Acidic runoff from mines created when water and oxygen react with sulfur-bearing minerals to produce sulfuric acid, which then leaches additional metals into the water.

acid rain
Precipitation containing higher than normal amounts of sulfuric acid and nitric acid, formed when natural rain-water combines with *sulfur dioxide and *nitrogen oxides emitted by burning of *fossil fuels.

acoustic territory
The range of sounds a particular species of animal emits and responds to.

acre-foot
Quantity of water or other material required to cover one acre or area to a depth of one foot.

acrylonitrile butadiene styrene (ABS)

Thermoplastic used to make vent and drainage pipes, toys, and *consumer goods.

activated carbon

A form of carbon processed at high temperatures to create small pores and thus increased surface area, making it highly adsorbent. Also known as activated charcoal. *See also* adsorption. *Compare* biochar.

activated sludge

(wastewater treatment) Suspended solids that contain high concentrations of aerobic bacteria which break down organic contaminants.

active solar heating

A system that uses mechanical devices such as pumps or fans to move heated air or liquid between solar collectors and a building.

actor

A person who participates in or has some influence on a process.

acute exposure

Short-term *exposure to high *doses of a *toxicant. *Compare* chronic effect.

adaptation

Adjustment in natural or human systems to a new or changing environment.

adaptive capacity

The ability of a system or community to adjust to change successfully.

adaptive cycles

Four phases of organization and function in system dynamics studied in relation to *resilience: rapid growth, conservation, release, and reorganization.

adaptive governance

A collaborative, flexible *governance approach based on self-organizing networks of people and *organizations and multiple scales.

adaptive management

(ecology) An iterative approach to managing resources that emphasizes experimentation, learning, and adjusting policies and practices in response to new information.

adaptive reuse

The practice of reusing a building or site for a purpose other than that for which it was originally designed.

adiabatic

A process in which heat is not gained or lost by the system.

adobe

A mixture of clay and straw, sun-dried and used to construct buildings.

adsorption

The adhesion of liquids, gases, or suspended matter to a surface.

advanced framing

A collection of framing techniques that reduce the amount of wood used and waste generated in wood-frame home construction.

advection

The transport of matter in a moving fluid.

adventure playground

An enclosed play area supplied with scrap materials and fasteners that children can use and tools they can borrow, facilitated by trained playworkers who provide materials, lend tools, and administer risk management protocols.

aerobic

Living systems or processes that occur in the presence of oxygen.

aerobic digestion
Treatment of *sludge involving *decomposition of organic matter by *aerobic bacteria. *See also* digestion.

aerosol
Minute solid or liquid airborne particle that remains suspended in the *atmosphere for at least several hours.

afforestation
The planting of new forest on land that historically has not been forested.

after-use pathway
The route a material travels during its *life cycle following its initial use.

agenda
A list of meeting topics. From the Latin word meaning "the things to be done."

Agenda 21
An action plan to promote sustainable development by addressing social, economic, and environmental impacts of human activity, adopted by delegates to the 1992 United Nations Conference on Environment and Development, or Earth Summit, in Rio de Janeiro.

age pyramid *See* age structure diagram.

age structure
The relative numbers of people of each gender at each age level within a *population.

age structure diagram
A diagram illustrating the age distribution of a *population, where the width of each bar corresponds to the number of individuals in each age class and gender.

aggradation
The filling of a stream channel as sediment is deposited.

aggregate
Coarse particles of rock, used in concrete and paving.

agribusiness *See* industrialized agriculture.

agricultural revolution
The shift from a hunter-gatherer lifestyle to an agricultural way of life with the dawn of the *Holocene epoch beginning around 12,000 years ago.

agriculture
The practice of cultivating plants and animals as food crops.

agriculture, sustainable *See* sustainable agriculture.

agriculture, traditional *See* traditional agriculture.

agroecology
An interdisciplinary approach which applies principles of ecology to the practice of *agriculture.

agroecosystem
The unit of study in agroecology; a site or landscape where agricultural production is understood as an *ecosystem.

agroforestry
The *intercropping of annual or perennial agricultural crops with trees or other woody plants.

A horizon
The top layer of soil. Also known as *topsoil. *See also* soil horizon.

AHU *See* air handling unit.

air change
The exchange of air in a building or space in which all of the interior air is replaced by outdoor air; the volume of one air change is equal to the interior volume of the building or space.

air changes per hour (ACH)
The number of complete *air changes within a given space in one hour.

air cleaning
The removal of pollutants from indoor air, typically using particulate filtration, electrostatic precipitation, or gas *sorption.

air conditioning
The process of cooling and dehumidifying indoor air for human comfort by mechanical methods such as a refrigeration unit or chilled water system. *See also* conditioned air.

air exchange rate
The rate at which interior air in a building or space is replaced by outdoor air, measured either in cubic feet per minute or *air changes per hour.

air handling unit (AHU)
Commercial device for distributing warm or cool air through a building; includes a blower or fan, heat-exchange coils, controls, and filters. Also known as an air handler.

air pollution
Airborne pollutants in concentrations high enough to cause harm to living organisms or materials.

air quality
Measurement of the health-related and visual characteristics of the air to which humans and the environment are exposed.

albedo
A measure of a surface's ability to reflect solar radiation, often expressed as a decimal fraction on a scale of 0 to 1. Generally, dark-colored surfaces have low albedo and light-colored surfaces have high albedo. Also known as solar reflectance. *See also* pyranometer.

algae
Single-celled or multi-celled organisms which carry out photosynthesis but are not plants.

algal bloom
Excessive growth of algae that depletes oxygen in a body of water; usually caused by excess nutrient inputs.

alien species *See* nonnative species.

alkaline
Having a *pH greater than 7; a substance that accepts *hydrogen ions. *Compare* acidic.

allergen
A substance that activates the body's immune system, causing a response when a response is not necessary.

alloy
A combination of two or more metals or a metal and another element.

alluvial deposit
Soil material deposited by running water.

alternating current (AC)
Electric *current produced by a spinning *generator in which charges reverse direction at regularly recurring intervals. *Compare* direct current.

alternative energy
An energy source that is an alternative to fossil fuels.

alternative fuel
A *fuel that is substantially not petroleum.

alternative transportation
Any transportation mode which does not involve a single-occupant vehicle powered by fossil fuel.

altitude angle
An angle in a vertical plane between the horizontal ground plane and a ray from the sun, indicating the height of the sun in the sky.

ambient
Conditions in the surrounding *environment.

ambient air
The surrounding *atmosphere.

ambient light
Light in the surrounding *environment that produces general illumination.

ambient sound
Sound from external sources out of one's control.

ambient temperature
The temperature of the surrounding *environment.

American National Standards Institute (ANSI)
A nonprofit *organization that administers and coordinates the US voluntary standardization system; the US representative to ISO.

amino acid
One of a group of *organic compounds which are the basic building blocks of protein in all living organisms.

anadromous
Marine species that spawn in freshwater streams, such as salmon.

anaerobic
Living systems or processes that occur in the absence of oxygen.

anaerobic digestion
Treatment of *sludge involving *decomposition of organic matter by *anaerobic bacteria. *See also* digestion.

analogy
A comparison of two things in different domains which suggests that if they are similar in some respects, they may be similar in other respects. *Compare* metaphor.

analysis
The separation of a whole into individual parts in order to learn about their nature, function, and relationship with other parts. *Compare* synthesis.

animal
A multicellular organism that meets its energy needs by eating other organisms.

animal rights
An area of focus within *environmental ethics which considers the *intrinsic value of animals independent of their usefulness to humans and their right not to suffer.

animism
From *anima*, the Latin word for "soul." The philosophy that all matter, both animate and inanimate, has an inner spirit. *Compare* organicism; pantheism.

anoxic
Lacking in or greatly deficient in oxygen.

ANSI *See* American National Standards Institute.

anthracite
A hard, black, lustrous coal; also known as hard coal.

Anthropocene epoch
Informal term for the most recent geological *epoch in Earth's history, beginning *c.*1800 CE around the start of the *Industrial Revolution. Formal designation is under consideration by the *International Commission on Stratigraphy.

anthropocentric
Biased in favor of the human species.

anthropocentrism
A view of reality in which human values and interests are primary.

anthropogenic
Resulting from human activities.

anthroposphere
The environment made by or modified by humans, including culture, technology, and the built environment.

appliance
Any energy-consuming device used in homes for purposes other than heating, cooling, or water heating.

appropriate technology
Technology that is small-scale, simple, and environmentally benign.

**appropriation
(of ecosystem services)**
The process of accessing or using the benefits provided by *ecosystem services.

aquaculture
The industrial farming of fish or seafood.

Aquaculture Stewardship Council (ASC)
*Organization that develops *certification standards and provides *eco-labels for farmed seafood. *Compare* Marine Stewardship Council.

aquifer
An underground water-bearing layer of permeable rock, sand, or gravel capable of supplying wells or springs.

arable land
Land that can be cultivated to grow crops.

Aral Sea
A saltwater lake in Central Asia, formerly the fourth largest lake in the world; now almost vanished because water was diverted for cotton production.

Archaea
Single-celled microorganisms lacking cell nuclei; one of the three primary *domains of life. Archaea and *bacteria are *prokaryotes. *Compare* eukaryote. *See also* bacteria.

Architecture 2030
Nonprofit *organization established in response to the global climate-change crisis, with the goal of achieving carbon neutrality in the building industry by 2030.

arid
A region characterized by a relative lack of precipitation hindering or preventing the growth and development of plant and animal life. *See also* desert.

array *See* photovoltaic array.

arsenic
A *heavy metal and *neurotoxin, sometimes present as a water pollutant.

artesian well
A well from which water flows naturally because of internal pressure in an *aquifer.

asbestos
A family of naturally occurring silicate minerals that forms microscopic fibers which can embed in lungs and lead to lung disease.

ASC *See* Aquaculture Stewardship Council.

ash
The mineral content of a product which remains after complete *combustion.

ASHRAE
American Society of Heating, Refrigerating and Air-Conditioning Engineers. An international *organization which establishes standards for heating, ventilation, air conditioning, and refrigeration.

aspect
The compass direction in which a slope or building faces. *See also* orientation.

asphalt
A dark, *cement-like material made primarily of bitumen, obtained by processing *petroleum. Also, a mixture of bituminous material and *aggregate used for paving.

asset
An *economic resource; anything which has monetary or exchange value.

assisted migration
The moving of *species to new regions with the goal of helping them to adapt to *climate change.

ASTM
The American Society for Testing and Materials. The *organization which develops US testing protocols and standards for characteristics of materials.

Atlantic gyre
A circular ocean current in Atlantic Ocean. *See also* gyre.

atmosphere
The mixture of gases surrounding the Earth, consisting primarily of nitrogen and oxygen with trace amounts of water vapor, aerosols, and other gases.

atmospheric lifetime
The approximate amount of time it would take for an increment of *anthropogenic *greenhouse gas concentration to return to its natural level.

atom
The smallest unit of matter that maintains the chemical properties of an element.

atomic number
The number of *protons in the nucleus of an *atom, which determines the chemical identity of the atom. All atoms of a particular element have the same atomic number.

atrium
A large enclosed space in a building for providing natural daylight. *Compare* light well.

attenuation
A reduction in force, value, intensity, or concentration.

attribute
A qualitative characteristic.

attribution
(climate science) Evaluation of the relative contributions of various causal factors to a change or event. *Compare* detection.

audit
A systematic process for collecting evidence to determine the extent to which certain criteria have been met. *See also* energy audit.

autopoiesis
The property of every living *system from a single *cell to a multicellular organism which allows it to regenerate and to reproduce itself. From the Greek words *auto-*, "self," and *poiesis*, "making."

autotroph

An organism that uses solar or *chemical energy to produce its own food. Also known as a *producer.

avoided cost

1 (ecology) The costs that would have been incurred in the absence of *ecosystem services or an environmental improvement.

2 (energy) The capital and operating costs a utility would have incurred for additional power had it built new facilities itself, versus purchasing power from another party.

axial tilt

The angle between Earth's axis of rotation and a line perpendicular to the plane of its orbit around the sun. The angle varies over a period of 41,000 years and is currently about 23.4°. *See also* Milankovitch cycles.

azimuth

1 A horizontal angle expressed in degrees.

2 The horizontal angle between true south and a point on the horizon directly below the sun.

B

backcasting
A planning approach which begins by envisioning a desired future, then works backward from that vision to develop strategies. *Compare* forecasting.

backflow
The unwanted reversal of water flow from its intended direction of flow. *See also* back pressure.

backflow preventer
A method or device designed to prevent *backflow via an air gap, vacuum breaker, or double check valve.

background extinction
The average rate of *extinction that has occurred over *geologic time. *Compare* mass extinction.

back pressure
A condition in which the pressure in a nonpotable system is greater than the pressure in a *potable water supply system. Can result in *backflow.

bacteria
Single-celled microorganisms lacking cell nuclei; one of the three primary domains of life. Archaea and bacteria are *prokaryotes. *Compare* eukaryote. *See also* Archaea.

baghouse
A system of large filters made of fabric used to remove *particulates.

balance of system
The components of a solar *photovoltaic system other than the panels themselves; consists of batteries, an *inverter, and controls.

ballast
1 (paving) *Aggregate used as a base layer.
2 (shipping) Heavy material placed in the bottom of a ship to improve stability.
3 (lighting) A device to limit current flow when starting fluorescent lamps.

bankfull
The height of a stream which just begins to overflow its banks.

barrel (bbl)
A liquid volume equal to 42 US gallons, used to indicate quantities of *petroleum products.

barter
The exchange of goods or services directly without the use of money as a medium of exchange.

BAS *See* building automation system.

baseflow
Streamflow contributed by *groundwater, even during rainless periods.

Basel Convention
The 1992 Basel Convention on the Control of Transboundary Movements of Hazardous Wastes and their Disposal, developed to reduce the movement of *hazardous waste from industrialized countries to developing countries.

baseline
A *reference condition against which change is measured.

base load
Typical daily *electricity demand; the minimum amount of *electric power a *utility must provide constantly to the *grid. *Compare* peak load.

basic solution *See* alkaline.

basin of attraction
Mathematical term, also used in ecology to describe the stable states of a system that do not change until some *threshold is reached; often illustrated as a ball-in-a-basin metaphor.

BAT *See* best available technology.

battery-electric vehicle (BEV)
An all-electric vehicle driven by electric motors and powered solely by batteries; also known as an electric car. *See also* electric vehicle.

BAU *See* business as usual.

bbl
Abbreviation for *barrel. Stands for "blue barrel," the original standard container for oil.

BCE
Abbreviation for Before the Common Era. A nonreligious term used in place

of BC (before Christ) to describe the period of time before year 1. *See also* CE.

BCF *See* bioconcentration factor.

B Corp *See* benefit corporation.

bearing
(surveying) A horizontal angle expressed in degrees, minutes, and seconds from either north or south toward the east or west.

bed load
Sediment that is too heavy to remain suspended and thus moves on or near the bottom of a stream.

bedrock
Solid rock underlying other unconsolidated material such as soil and subsoil. Also known as the *R horizon.

behavior change
A change in activity which is under the control of an individual. *Compare* social change; structural change.

benchmark
A reference point from which performance or trends can be measured. *See also* baseline.

benefit
A profit, advantage, or positive change in well-being.

benefit corporation (B Corp)
A form of corporation established under corporate law which permits the use of business profits for social and environmental benefit. *Compare* corporation.

benthic
Related to or living on the bottom of a water body.

bentonite
A clay that expands when wet, used for liners and covers in landfills and ponds.

berm
A linear mound of soil or sand, either naturally occurring or constructed.

Best Available Technology (BAT)
The most effective, economically achievable technique for preventing or treating pollution.

best management practice (BMP)
Measures determined to be effective and used to prevent or reduce water pollution.

Betz's Law
The theoretical maximum efficiency of wind turbines, which can extract no more than 59.3% of the energy in wind regardless of wind turbine design.

BEV *See* battery-electric vehicle.

BHAG
Acronym for "Big, Hairy, Audacious Goal," an informal term used in planning to refer to an ambitious goal.

Bhopal
A city in India that was the site of a massive insecticide spill in 1984 which killed thousands of people.

B horizon
The layer of soil below the *A horizon. Also known as *subsoil. *See also* soil horizon.

bi-fuel vehicle
A vehicle which can operate on either one of two different fuels, stored in separate tanks and not mixed. *See also* dual-fuel vehicle.

big history
A study of history at multiple temporal and spatial scales, including human history and cosmology.

binary geothermal system
A geothermal power system that uses hot water to heat a second working fluid which then drives a turbine.

bioaccumulation
The process in which the concentration of a substance taken in by an organism increases faster than the rate at which the organism can remove it.

bioattenuation
The use of indigenous microorganisms and nutrients on site to break down pollutants. Also known as intrinsic, natural, or passive *bioremediation.

bioaugmentation
The inoculation of a polluted site with additional microorganisms to promote *bioremediation.

bio-based
A material derived from a biological source.

biocapacity
The capacity of *ecosystems to produce useful biological materials and to absorb waste materials generated by humans, using current management schemes and extraction technologies.

biocentrism
A view of reality in which the values and interests of non-human life are primary.

biochar
Carbon residue made by burning *biomass in the absence of oxygen at relatively low temperatures; also known as *charcoal. *See also* pyrolysis.

biochemical oxygen demand (BOD)
A measure of organic content in water, given by the amount of dissolved oxygen consumed by aquatic organisms as they break down organic matter.

bioconcentration
The accumulation of a *chemical in an aquatic organism where the chemical

concentration in the organism is greater than the surrounding water.

bioconcentration factor (BCF)
The ratio of the concentration of a *chemical in an aquatic organism to the concentration in the surrounding water.

biodegradable
Capable of being broken down into simpler substances by microorganisms.

biodiesel
A fuel made of oils from plant materials or animal fats and used as a diesel fuel substitute or diesel fuel extender.

biodiversity
The variety of genes, species, and *ecosystems found in a given area.

biodiversity hotspot
One of several areas that contains an especially great diversity of endemic species facing a high risk of extinction.

bioenergy
Energy derived from biomass such as recently living organisms or their metabolic by-products.

biofilm
A layer of microorganisms attached to surfaces.

biofiltration
The use of vegetation and microorganisms to capture and biologically degrade pollutants.

biofuel
A liquid fuel made of plant material and used as a partial substitute for gasoline.

biogas
A gas generated by the decomposition of *organic waste. *See also* landfill gas.

biogeochemical cycle
The movement of matter in cycles through the *atmosphere, *lithosphere,

*hydrosphere, and *biosphere. *See also* carbon cycle; hydrologic cycle; nitrogen cycle.

biogeography
The study of the geographic distribution of organisms. *See also* island biogeography.

biointensive agriculture
An approach to producing high yields of food crops in small spaces using raised beds, compost, and densely planted crops; also known as French intensive agriculture.

biological control
The control of pests through the use of natural enemies.

biological diversity *See* biodiversity.

biological integrity index
A summary numeric that can be used to compare *ecosystem health in watersheds, based on species abundance.

biological metabolism
In *cradle-to-cradle systems, the cycle in which *biological nutrients flow. *Compare* technical metabolism.

biological nutrient
A product made of materials designed to return to the *biosphere. *See also* cradle to cradle; biological metabolism.

biological pump
The process in which dead photosynthetic marine organisms sink and transport carbon from the ocean's surface layers to the deep ocean.

biological treatment
The treatment of *wastewater using *aerobic bacteria.

biomagnification
The process in which the concentration of a substance increases as it passes

to successively higher *trophic levels of a *food web.

biomass
1 (biology) The total weight of all living organisms in a particular area.
2 (energy) Plant or animal material, often wood or grasses, that can be converted into energy through burning or through conversion into a gas or liquid *fuel which is then burned.

biomass, traditional
The use of wood, charcoal, *agricultural residues, and animal dung for cooking and *heating in developing countries.

biome
A major regional habitat type characterized by particular climate and soil conditions and particular biological communities.

biomimicry
An approach to designing products or buildings using nature as a model.

biophilia
The genetically encoded emotional need of human beings to affiliate with nature and with other living organisms, rooted in human biology and evolution.

biophilic design
An approach to designing the built environment in ways that connect people with the natural world.

biophysical
Related to the living and nonliving components and processes of the *biosphere.

bioplastic
A biodegradable *plastic made from plant material.

biopower
*Electricity generated by *biomass.

bioregion
A geographical area, all of which has similar *climate, *topography, plant, and animal communities.

bioregionalism
An approach to living and learning which is based on local knowledge of the particular bioregion where a person or group of people live. See also place-based learning.

bioremediation
The use of microorganisms, *fungi, or plants to break down *pollutants in *soil or water.

biosolids
*Sewage sludge that has been treated to stabilize or remove *pollutants and *pathogens.

biosphere
The part of the *Earth system on land, in the oceans, and in the *atmosphere inhabited by living organisms.

biostimulation
The addition of nutrients to stimulate bacterial action.

bioswale
A vegetated linear depression used to cleanse and *infiltrate *stormwater. See also swale.

biosyngas See synthetic gas.

biota
All living organisms in a given area.

biotic
Living. Compare abiotic.

biotope
A local area that supports a particular range of biological communities.

bioventing
The use of pressure to force *oxygen into soil to aid *aerobic bacteria in breaking down *pollutants.

BIPV *See* building integrated photovoltaics.

bird-friendly design
Strategies to break up reflections in window glass so that birds are less likely to collide with windows.

birth rate
The total number of people born in a given year. *See also* fertility rate; replacement fertility rate.

bisphenol-A (BPA)
A chemical additive found in thermal cash register receipts and added to some *polycarbonates and other *plastics including food packaging; known to be a *mutagen and *endocrine disruptor.

bitumen
A black, high-*viscosity oil extracted from *tar sands or obtained as a residue of *petroleum distillation. *See also* asphalt.

bituminous coal
A dense, black, soft *coal; used for generating *electricity, making *coke, and heating.

black carbon
Dark particulate matter formed by the incomplete *combustion of *fossil fuels, biofuels, and *biomass. Also known as soot. *Compare* carbon black.

black swan event
A metaphor for an event that is unexpected and has major impact.

blackwater
*Wastewater which contains feces, urine, or food *waste; includes wastewater from toilets, kitchen sinks, and dishwashers.

blade
The aerodynamic structure on a *wind turbine that catches the wind.

bleach
To treat textile or wood pulp fibers chemically for the purpose of removing color and residual *lignins such as bark.

bleaching, coral *See* coral bleaching.

bloom *See* algal bloom.

blowdown *See* cooling tower blowdown water.

blowing agent
A chemical agent used to create a cellular structure in *plastics or other materials; used for making foam.

blue-green algae
Former and inaccurate name for *cyanobacteria.

Blue Marble
Informal name given to a 1972 photograph of Earth taken from the Apollo 17 moon rocket.

blue water
Freshwater in *aquifers, rivers, and lakes. *See also* green water.

BMP *See* best management practice.

BOD *See* biochemical oxygen demand.

BOD5
The *biochemical oxygen demand of *wastewater during *decomposition occurring over a 5-day period.

bog
A *wetland with no significant inflows or outflows that accumulates *peat.

boreal forest
Coniferous *forest *biome covering the northern latitudes of North America and Eurasia. Also known as taiga.

borrow pit
An area from which *soil, *sand, or gravel are excavated for use elsewhere.

borrow–use–return
An informal name for *closed-loop models such as those found in *cradle-to-cradle systems. *Compare* take–make–waste.

bottle bill
Legislation that requires a returnable deposit on beverage containers.

bottled water
Drinking water sold in plastic or glass bottles.

bottom ash
Remaining noncombustible material that collects at the bottom of a *combustion chamber. *Compare* fly ash.

bottoming cycle
A *combined-heat-and-power system in which heat is the primary product and *electricity is the secondary product. *See also* topping cycle.

bottom trawling
Fishing practice in which trawlers drag nets, chains, and weights across the seafloor in order to trap fish. *See also* trawl.

boundaries, planetary *See* planetary boundaries.

box scheme
European name for *community-supported agriculture.

BP
Abbreviation for Before Present. Since the present is a moving marker, 1950 *CE is used as the year from which BP dates are counted.

BPA *See* bisphenol-A.

brackish
A mix of *fresh water and salt water.

braided
A stream channel that forms secondary or smaller side channels.

brainstorming
A *group process for generating ideas spontaneously and without evaluation.

BREEAM
The Building Research Establishment Environmental Assessment Method, a green building rating system developed in the UK and used in Europe. *Compare* LEED.

BRIC
Acronym for Brazil, Russia, India, China.

BRIICS
Acronym for Brazil, Russia, India, Indonesia, China, and South Africa.

British thermal unit (Btu)
The quantity of *heat required to raise the *temperature of 1 pound of water by 1 degree Fahrenheit at or near 39.2 degrees Fahrenheit.

brood parasite
A bird that lays its eggs in the nest of another bird, which then cares for the offspring.

brown bag lunch
An informal, voluntary meeting held during an employee break such as a lunch break.

brown cloud
Informal name for *photochemical smog.

brownfield
An abandoned or under-used industrial site in which redevelopment or reuse is complicated by the presence or potential presence of a hazardous material.

BRT *See* bus rapid transit.

Brundtland Commission
Informal name for the *World Commission on Environment and Development created by the *UN in 1983.

Btu *See* British thermal unit.

buffer
A zone or strip of land between one land use and another to minimize negative impacts.

buildable land
An unoccupied portion of a site that is suitable for construction.

building automation system (BAS)
A computerized network of electronic devices designed to monitor and control a building's *mechanical and lighting systems.

building code
The legal requirements concerning the building of structures enacted by a jurisdiction for the protection of public health and safety.

building envelope *See* envelope.

building integrated photovoltaics (BIPV)
*Photovoltaic modules that are integrated into a building *envelope to provide enclosure while generating *electricity.

building-related illness
An illness with symptoms which can be clinically defined and which have known identifiable causes which can be attributed directly to airborne building contaminants. *Compare* sick building syndrome.

bulk density
A measure of soil compaction, expressed as dry weight of the soil per unit volume.

bunker fuel
Heavy, residual fuel oil left after petroleum distillation typically used to power cargo ship engines.

bureaucracy
A system of administration organized as a hierarchy with fixed rules and procedures.

business as usual (BAU)
The condition in which operating practices and policies remain as they are at present.

business case
A quantitative assessment of the opportunities and risks connected with a proposed plan, used for making a business decision.

bus rapid transit (BRT)
Public transportation system using buses which combine features of bus and rail including frequent service, large capacity, dedicated travel lanes, traffic signal priority, and quick passenger loading and unloading from accessible, platform-level doors.

butterfly effect
The idea expressed in *chaos theory that a very small change in a complex system can result in large effects.

by-catch
Animals caught unintentionally during commercial fishing.

by-product
An incidental or secondary product of a manufacturing process or *chemical reaction.

C

CAFE *See* Corporate Average Fuel Economy.

CAFO *See* concentrated animal feeding operation.

calcination
The use of heat to solidify wastes.

calibration
The practice of taking measurements in relation to some specified standard in order to determine accuracy.

caliche
A hardened, light-colored layer of calcium carbonate in soils of arid regions.

calving
The breaking off of pieces of ice from the edge of a glacier, ice sheet, or ice shelf into water, producing *icebergs.

cancer cluster
A greater-than-expected number of cancer cases, usually associated with exposures to toxins in the workplace.

candela (cd)
A measure of the luminous intensity of a light source in the SI system. *See also* candlepower.

candlepower (cp)
A measure of the luminous intensity of a light source; the result of 1 *foot-candle of illumination over a surface which is 1 foot from the source. *See also* candela.

canola
A variety of rapeseed, used to make edible oil and biodiesel.

canopy
The uppermost layer of tree vegetation.

capacity building
A process of developing or strengthening human resources, *organizations, and *social capital.

capacity factor
The ratio of the electrical energy produced for a given period of time to the electrical energy that could have been produced at continuous full-power operation during the same period.

cap and trade
The buying and selling of permits to pollute; also known as *emissions trading.

capital
The supply of resources available. *See also* natural capital; social capital.

capitalism
An economic system of private ownership of the means of production conducted to gain a profit.

capital project
A long-term investment in the improvement of a fixed asset, such as a building or *infrastructure, requiring a comparatively high financial outlay.

captive breeding
The practice of breeding captive animals in controlled environments such as zoos or wildlife centers, often as part of conservation efforts. *See also* introduction; reintroduction.

carbon black
A form of carbon produced commercially and used as pigment. *Compare* black carbon.

carbon capture and sequestration (CCS)
Technology which removes carbon dioxide from industrial processes and stores it underground or under the ocean floor. *Compare* carbon sequestration.

carbon credit
A tradeable financial unit of measure that represents carbon dioxide or carbon dioxide equivalent removed or reduced. Also known as a *carbon offset.

carbon cycle
The sum of the processes by which carbon continuously cycles between the *atmosphere, *biosphere, *hydrosphere, and *lithosphere.

carbon dioxide (CO_2)
A naturally occurring gas used by plants for *photosynthesis and given off by

*respiration of animals; also a by-product of burning *fossil fuels and *biomass, *land-use changes, and industrial processes. The principal *anthropogenic *greenhouse gas.

carbon dioxide equivalent (CO_2e)
The climate impact of a *greenhouse gas expressed as the tons of carbon dioxide that would result in the same impact; determined by multiplying the tons of the given gas by its *global warming potential.

carbon dioxide fertilization
An increase in the growth rate of plants as a result of increased atmospheric carbon dioxide concentration.

carbon farming
Farming practices which sequester carbon.

carbon flux
The rate of exchange of carbon between *reservoirs.

carbon footprint
A measure of *greenhouse gas emissions associated with an activity; technically the area of land needed for *carbon sequestration for a particular activity, but often used more loosely to mean the quantity of greenhouse gases emitted, measured in tons of carbon dioxide equivalent. *See also* ecological footprint.

carbon intensity
The relative amount of carbon by weight emitted per unit of energy consumed.

carbon leakage
The situation in which businesses transfer production to regions with less stringent climate policies.

carbon monoxide (CO)
A colorless, odorless gas and *pollutant which results from incomplete *combustion of *fossil fuels.

carbon neutral
Living or doing business in a way that results in no net carbon emissions; also known as *climate neutral.

carbon offset See offset.

carbon pool
A *reservoir containing carbon as a principal element in the geochemical cycle.

carbon pricing
Placing a price on carbon *pollution through either *emissions trading or *carbon taxes as a means of reducing emissions.

carbon sequestration
The removal and storage of carbon in a *carbon sink through biological or physical processes. *Compare* carbon capture and sequestration.

carbon sink
A reservoir that absorbs carbon from another part of the carbon cycle, such as *forests, oceans, *atmosphere, and *soil.

carbon tax
A levy on the carbon content of *fossil fuel, usually based on CO_2 emissions. *See also* carbon pricing.

carbon trading See emissions trading.

carcinogen
A substance known to increase the risk of developing cancer.

carpooling
The travel of two or more people in the same vehicle.

carrying capacity
The maximum number of individuals that a given environment can support indefinitely.

car sharing
A program that provides the use of an automobile to more than one person, reducing the need for individual ownership.

CAS See complex adaptive system.

cash crop
A crop produced for profit rather than for consumption by the people who grew it.

CAS number
Chemical Abstract Service number, a unique identifier assigned to nearly every known chemical substance.

catalyst
A substance that facilitates or accelerates a *chemical reaction without undergoing permanent chemical change itself.

catalytic converter
A device on a vehicle exhaust *system that converts *pollutants into less *toxic *emissions.

catch basin
A drainage-system receptacle with a *sump in which sediment settles out before water is diverted to a subsurface pipe.

catchment
1   A *watershed.
2   The roof area which collects water for a *rainwater harvesting system.

CCS See carbon capture and sequestration.

cd See candela.

CDD See cooling degree day.

C&D waste See construction and demolition waste.

CE
Abbreviation for Common Era. A non-religious term used in place of AD (*Anno Domini*) to describe the period of time beginning in year 1. *See also* BCE.

cell
1   (biology) The smallest organizational unit of life; all cells are

surrounded by *membranes, have *metabolisms, and are able to duplicate themselves.

2 (computer modeling) In a *climate model, the smallest division of Earth's surface, *atmosphere, or ocean.

cell, landfill *See* landfill cell.

cell, photovoltaic *See* photovoltaic cell.

cellulose
A naturally occurring *polymer that is the principal structural constituent of the *cell walls of plants.

cellulosic ethanol
Ethanol produced from the *cellulose in plant tissues, often grasses.

cement
A mixture of limestone and other minerals processed at high temperatures and used to bind the constituents of *concrete.

centralized power
Power produced by a *utility which enters a user's site at a meter. *Compare* distributed power.

CERCLA
The Comprehensive Environmental Response, Compensation, and Liability Act, a US law which regulates *wastes on land and in navigable waters; also known as *Superfund.

certification
A procedure by which a *third party verifies the level of performance of a product, process, or service compared to some standard.

CFC *See* chlorofluorocarbon.

CFL *See* compact fluorescent light.

cfm
Cubic feet per minute.

chain of custody
The tracing of a product or commodity through every step of its supply chain as part of *certification.

champion
A person who takes interest in a cause or project and leads change on its behalf in an *organization.

change agent
A person who plays a central role in the initiation and shaping of processes of *transformation.

channel
The part of a *stream where water collects to flow downstream including the streambed and streambanks.

channelization
The human engineering of a stream channel such as straightening, enlarging, or embanking.

chaos theory
The mathematical theory that very small changes in the initial state of a system lead to large and unpredictable effects. *See also* butterfly effect; nonlinearity.

chaotic
The characteristic of a *system in which very small changes lead to large, unpredictable changes in the system's trajectory. *See also* nonlinearity.

chaparral
A *biome consisting of evergreen shrubs found in Mediterranean climates.

characterization
The step in a pollution *remediation project in which the magnitude and extent of impact are determined.

charcoal
Carbon residue made by burning *biomass in the absence of oxygen at

relatively low temperatures; also known as *biochar. *See also* pyrolysis.

charge *See* electrical charge.

charrette
A fast-paced planning process in which participation by multiple *stakeholders produces a collaborative solution.

check dam
A small water control structure constructed across a *swale or channel, used to slow the velocity of water, reduce *erosion, and allow *sediment to settle out.

chemical
A substance produced by or used in a reaction involving changes to the bonds between *atoms; a substance represented by a single *CAS number.

Chemical Abstract Service *See* CAS number.

chemical energy
*Potential energy stored in chemical bonds between *atoms.

chemical reaction
An interaction between *chemicals in which there is a change in the chemical composition of the elements or compounds involved.

chemical recycling
An approach to *recycling *plastic *waste in which *polymers are broken down into individual *monomers or other chemical feedstock which are used to produce new polymers. *See also* depolymerization.

chemical sensitivity *See* multiple chemical sensitivity.

Chernobyl
The site of a *nuclear power plant in the Ukraine where a nuclear reactor exploded in 1986.

child labor
Work that is mentally, physically, socially, or morally dangerous and harmful to children and that interferes with their schooling.

chilled beam
A *radiant cooling device in which cold water circulates through tubes, usually in the ceiling.

chiller
A commercial-scale mechanical device that uses refrigeration to chill water for space cooling.

chimney effect *See* stack effect.

chlorofluorocarbon (CFC)
One of a group of chemical compounds containing atoms of carbon, chlorine, and fluorine that are harmful to the *ozone layer of the *atmosphere. *See also* Montreal Protocol.

chlorophyll
A molecule found in the *chloroplasts of plant cells that enables *photosynthesis.

chloroplast
An energy-transformation organelle in a plant cell where *photosynthesis occurs.

choice editing
An approach which removes the most environmentally or socially damaging products from the market, pre-selecting the range of products available to *consumers.

C horizon
The layer of soil below the *B horizon, consisting of unweathered parent material and relatively devoid of organic material. *See also* soil horizon.

choropleth map
A map showing areas of various sizes and shapes representing qualitative or

quantitative phenomena; often has a mosaic appearance.

CHP *See* combined heat and power.

chronic exposure
Long-term *exposure to low *doses of a *toxicant. *Compare* acute exposure.

circadian rhythm
Changes in the physiological processes of most organisms that follow a roughly 24-hour cycle, responding primarily to light and darkness in the organism's environment.

circular economy
A *closed-loop economy with a continuous cyclic flow of materials, where output from one process becomes input for another. *See also* cradle to cradle; zero waste.

cistern
A container for storing water, often rainwater.

CITES
The Convention on International Trade in Endangered Species of Wild Fauna and Flora; an international agreement administered by *UNEP to ensure that international trade in specimens of wild animals and plants does not threaten their survival.

clarifier
A settling tank in which solids are separated from treated *wastewater.

clarity *See* turbidity.

classical economics
The study of macroeconomics, or the economy as a whole. *Compare* neoclassical economics.

clathrate
A substance in which one molecule type forms a crystal-like cage structure and encloses another type of molecule. *See also* hydrate; methane hydrate.

clay
Soil with particles less than 0.002 mm in size; often consists of silicates and metal oxides. *See also* soil texture.

clean coal
Attempts to mitigate impacts of coal-burning through the use of technology such as gasification and *carbon capture and sequestration.

cleanup
Action taken to remediate the impacts of release of a *hazardous substance.

clearcut
An area in which all of the trees in a forest stand have been cut regardless of size.

clerestory
Vertical window openings near a roof.

CLFR *See* compact linear Fresnel reflector.

climate
Long-term trends in temperature, precipitation, and wind measured over decades, centuries, or longer. *Compare* weather.

climate action plan
A formal program to reduce an *organization's or community's *climate impact.

climate change
A significant change in measures of climate such as temperature, precipitation, and wind lasting for an extended period of time; can result from natural processes or human activity.

climate commitment
The climate change that would still occur even with no further human influence, resulting from greenhouse gases already emitted.

climate drawdown
The point at which *greenhouse gas concentrations in the *atmosphere begin to decline year to year.

climate feedback
An interaction mechanism between processes in the *climate system in which the result of an initial process triggers changes in a second process that in turn influences the initial one. *See also* feedback.

climate forcing *See* radiative forcing.

climate justice
The concept that the burdens and benefits of *climate change and its impacts should be shared equitably.

climate lag
The delay that occurs in *climate change as a result of some factor that changes very slowly.

climate model
A computerized simulation of how the various parts of the *climate system interact with each other.

climate neutral
Living or doing business in a way which results in no net climate impact; also known as *carbon neutral.

climate proxy *See* proxy.

climate sensitivity
A measure of the strengths of the *feedbacks at a particular time; the proportional change in surface temperature following a change in *radiative forcing.

climate skepticism
A term loosely used to describe the views of people who do not accept scientific evidence about global *climate change.

climate system
The complex *system consisting of five major components of the *Earth system that are responsible for the climate and its variations: the *atmosphere, the *hydrosphere, the *cryosphere, the *lithosphere, and the *biosphere, and the interactions between them.

climax community
Historic term for a *community resulting from a process of ecological *succession that remains unchanged in the absence of *disturbance.

closed loop
A cyclical system of production in which the concept of waste is eliminated. *See also* circular economy; cradle to cradle; zero waste.

closed-loop cooling system
In a *thermoelectric power plant, a system that circulates water between a steam condenser and a cooling tower, adding small amounts of *makeup water to replace water lost through evaporation. Also known as a wet-recirculating system. *Compare* dry cooling system.

closed system
A *system in which matter circulates within the system but does not flow through it.

cluster *See* galaxy cluster.

clustered development *See* conservation development.

CO$_2$ *See* carbon dioxide.

CO$_2$e *See* carbon dioxide equivalent.

coal
A solid *fossil fuel containing mostly carbon, produced when terrestrial plant material was buried and compressed

under high pressure and high *temperature conditions within the *crust.

coalbed methane
*Methane contained in *coal seams, formed from the same processes as *natural gas in oil fields.

coal gasification
The conversion of solid *coal to *synthetic *natural gas or other gaseous mixture that can be burned as a *fuel.

coal liquefaction
The conversion of solid coal to a liquid fuel such as *synthetic *crude oil or *methanol.

coal mine methane
*Coalbed methane that is released during the process of coal *mining.

coarse woody debris *See* large woody debris.

cob
A composite mixture of clay, *sand, straw, and water used as a building material which is built up by hand.

code *See* building code.

coefficient of runoff *See* runoff coefficient.

coevolution
A process in which changes in two or more *species affect each other's evolution.

cogeneration
The production of *electrical energy and heat from the same fuel or energy source. Also known as *combined heat and power.

cohousing
An *intentional community of private homes clustered around shared space with collaborative planning of *community activities.

coir
Brown fiber from coconut husks.

coke
A hard, porous *fuel of concentrated carbon made from processing bituminous *coal at high temperatures.

coliform *See* fecal coliform.

collaborative consumption *See* sharing economy.

collapse
A sudden and complete breakdown or failure.

collective learning
The ability to exchange large amounts of learned information precisely using symbolic language.

collector
An animal in an aquatic *food web who feeds on fine particulate organic matter. *Compare* grazer; shredder. *See also* solar collector.

colony collapse disorder
The phenomenon in which a majority of worker honeybees disappear from a hive.

combined heat and power (CHP)
The production of *electricity and useful heat using a common energy source. Formerly known as *cogeneration.

combined sewer overflow
An event that occurs when more rain falls than a storm-sewer system can accommodate, and raw *sewage overflows into a waterway before it can be treated.

combined sewer system
A single set of underground pipes which carry both *sewage and *stormwater.

combustion
Rapid chemical oxidation accompanied by the generation of *light and *heat.

command and control
A hierarchical approach to governance in which the governing authority commands actions to be taken and controls methods by which they are done; an approach with strict regulations.

commercial
A non-residential, non-industrial building sector that consists of businesses and all types of private and public institutions. *Compare* residential.

commingled recycling
A method of recycling *municipal solid waste in which all material considered recyclable is collected together. Also known as single-stream recycling.

comminuter
A machine that shreds or pulverizes solids to make waste treatment easier.

comminution
The mechanical shredding or pulverizing of waste in *solid waste management and in *wastewater treatment.

commissioning
The systematic process of verifying and documenting that building systems are functioning as intended.

commodity
An article of trade or commerce; often refers to an agricultural or mining product that can be processed and resold.

common pool resource (CPR)
A resource from which it is difficult to exclude or limit users and in which use of the resource by one person decreases the benefits for others. *See also* commons. *Compare* public good.

commons
A *common pool resource plus a *community plus a set of *protocols for managing the resource.

community
1 A group of interacting species living in a particular area.
2 A group of people inhabiting a particular place with shared cultural patterns, social relationships, and governance structures.

community currency *See* local currency.

community energy
An energy system in which the energy consumed in a community is owned and controlled by that community. *See also* distributed power; local energy.

community garden
A piece of land on which food is grown by a group of people.

community participation *See* public participation.

community solar
An installation in which *solar panels are owned by a local *utility, a non-profit *organization, or a collaboration of community members.

community-supported agriculture (CSA)
An approach to supplying food in which customers buy subscriptions to local farms in return for regular deliveries of shares of the harvests. *See also* box scheme; subscription farming.

compact fluorescent light (CFL)
A small fluorescent *lamp used as a replacement for a screw-in incandescent bulb.

compaction
A process in which particles of soil are pushed together and the pore spaces

between them are reduced in size or closed off.

compact linear Fresnel reflector (CLFR)

A type of *concentrating solar power similar to a *parabolic trough design but using flat parallel mirrors and Fresnel lenses.

companion planting

The planting of two or more species in proximity to increase yield or vigor or to control pests. See also polyculture.

competition

A relationship between two or more organisms who require the same limited resource.

complementarity

(economics) A relationship between two or more elements that must be used together or in which one element affects the value of the other. Compare substitutability.

complementary currency

A *local currency used in addition to an official government currency.

complete street

A street designed to be convenient and safe for all users, all travel modes, and all abilities. Also known as a *multiway boulevard.

complex adaptive system (CAS)

A *system of interconnected components with *emergent behavior and the capacity to adapt and self-organize in response to *disturbance or change.

complexity

A term used to characterize interacting relationships in a *nonlinear system in which interactions are *emergent and outcomes cannot be predicted. Compare reductionism.

compliance

The act of meeting all applicable *regulations.

complicated

Refers to a system with many parts where there are knowable causes and effects and outcomes can be predicted given enough information. Compare complexity.

compost

Decomposed organic matter which has been broken down by microorganisms in a controlled environment.

compostable

A material capable of undergoing biological *decomposition.

compost blanket

A layer of loosely applied composted material placed on the soil to promote *stormwater *infiltration and plant growth.

composting toilet

A system for treating human waste by *composting, using little or no water for flushing and no connection to a *sewer or *septic system.

compost tea

Liquid made by moving water through compost.

compound

A combination of two or more *elements held together by chemical bonds.

concentrated animal feeding operation (CAFO)

An industrial-scale facility for housing animals at high densities for feeding prior to slaughter; also known as a feedlot.

concentrating solar power (CSP)

A *thermoelectric power system that uses lenses or mirrors to capture and focus *solar radiation to provide heat for steam boilers. *See also* compact linear Fresnel reflector; dish concentrator; parabolic trough; heliostat; power tower.

concentration
The quantity of a *chemical within a particular volume or weight of air, water, soil, or other medium. *See also* ppb; ppm.

concentration time
The time required for a drop of rain to pass from the perimeter of a drainage basin to the outlet. Also known as time of concentration or travel time.

concept map
A graphic method of illustrating ideas and relationships, similar to a flowchart. *Compare* mind map.

concrete
A mixture of *cement, sand, coarse *aggregates, and water.

condensation
The change of state from gas to liquid when water vapor in air becomes liquid water, caused by a decrease in *temperature.

condenser
The *heat exchanger in a *heat pump or other refrigeration cycle that discharges heat to the outside environment. *See also* evaporator.

conditioned air
Indoor air that has been heated, cooled, humidified, or dehumidified to provide comfort.

conduction
The transfer of heat energy by direct contact between individual molecules. *Compare* convection; radiation.

conductivity
1 The degree to which a material conducts *electricity.
2 The rate at which heat flows through a material. *See also* conductor.

conductor
A material that allows electric *current to flow readily.

cone of depression
A localized concavity in the *water table around a pumping well. Also known as a drawdown cone.

Conference of the Parties
The supreme body of the *United Nations Framework Convention on Climate Change, which meets annually. *See also* COP21.

conifer
A cone-bearing plant with needle-shaped or scale-like leaves; most are *evergreens.

conjunctive use
A system of water management which alternates use of underground water stored in *groundwater banking with the use of surface water in lieu of groundwater pumping, so that neither *aquifers nor rivers are critically depleted.

connectivity
The way and degree to which resources or organisms move or interact among *habitats or *landscapes.

consensus
The outcome of a group decision-making process in which the views of each participant have been heard and considered and the resolution is one that can be supported by every participant. *See also* scientific consensus.

conservation

1 Activity to maintain *biodiversity and *ecosystem function in a particular area.
2 A term used in the early twentieth century to mean a view of nature as a resource to be efficiently managed for human use.

conservation agriculture

A collection of farming practices used together to improve soil health, improve rainwater *infiltration, and decrease *erosion including *no-till, *cover cropping, and *crop rotation.

conservation banking

A mechanism similar to wetland *mitigation banking in which *habitat areas are set aside to compensate for *habitat that is destroyed elsewhere; banked *habitats provide credits which can be bought and sold.

conservation biology

A scientific discipline that focuses on the preservation of *biodiversity.

conservation development

A subdivision in which development is concentrated more densely onto less ecologically important lands, leaving a larger proportion of *open space undeveloped. Also known as clustered development.

conservation easement

A legal agreement in which a landowner retains ownership of their property but permanently relinquishes the right to build on or develop the property, often in exchange for financial or tax benefit.

conservation of energy See thermodynamics, first law of.

conservation of matter

Physical law stating that matter can change form but that it cannot be created or destroyed.

conservation subdivision See conservation development.

conservation tillage

An approach to growing crops by planting in undisturbed soil covered by crop residues and other mulch. Also known as *no-till farming.

conservative species

A species with a very narrow tolerance for certain conditions.

constructed wetland

A *wetland feature engineered to use natural processes of plants, soils, and bacteria living in association with wetland plant roots for the purpose of water or *wastewater treatment.

construction and demolition (C&D) waste

Material left over from the construction, remodeling, repair, or demolition of structures.

consumables

Non-durable goods that are likely to be used up or depleted quickly.

consumer

1 (ecology) An organism that consumes plants or other photosynthesizers. Also known as a *heterotroph.
2 (economics) An individual who purchases and uses products and services.

consumption

The use of goods and services by households.

consumption-based accounting

A method of conducting *greenhouse gas inventories using the value of the goods traded as an alternative to production-based accounting approaches.

containment
The use of a physical barrier to prevent, or try to prevent, a *contaminant from moving.

contaminant
Any unwanted substance that has an adverse effect on air, water, or soil.

contaminant plume *See* plume.

contaminated land
Land that has been polluted with *hazardous materials and requires cleanup or *remediation.

continental drift
An element of the theory of *plate tectonics which says that continents are always in motion and not fixed.

continuous improvement
A management concept which involves steady progress and an ongoing cycle of planning, implementing, assessing, and adapting. *See also* environmental management systems; plan-do-check-act cycle.

contour
A line of equal elevation drawn on a map; an imaginary line of equal elevation on the ground.

contour farming
The practice of tilling across a slope, following *contour lines, in order to reduce *erosion and improve *infiltration.

contour interval
The difference in elevation between two adjacent *contours.

convection
The transfer of heat energy through motion within a *fluid. *Compare* conduction; radiation.

conventional oil
Free-flowing *petroleum extracted with conventional vertical drilling methods. *Compare* unconventional oil.

conventional pollutants
Major water pollutants regulated by the US Clean Water Act: *biochemical oxygen demand, *total suspended solids, *fecal coliform bacteria, *pH, and oil and grease.

conventional power
Power produced in *power plants from *fossil fuels, *nuclear energy, or *hydroelectric dams. *Compare* renewable energy.

conversion
A form of *recycling in which a material is reprocessed into a material of lower quality. *See* downcycling.

conveyor belt, global *See* thermohaline circulation.

cool roof
A roof covered with material which reflects rather than absorbs sunlight.

cooling degree day (CDD)
The number of degrees per day that the average 24-hour daily temperature is above 65°F, used to estimate cooling requirements.

cooling load
Heat gain; the rate at which *heat must be removed from a space to maintain constant *temperature and *humidity. *Compare* heating load.

cooling tower
A structure in which heat is removed from water that has been used as a coolant.

cooling tower blowdown
Water released from a *cooling tower to maintain proper water mineral *concentration.

cooling tower makeup water

Water added to a *cooling tower to replace water lost to evaporation or blowdown.

coolth

The absence of heat.

cool tower

A passive down-draft tower in which hot dry air meets evaporating water on a wet pad at the top, is cooled and becomes heavier, and falls to an outlet at the bottom.

cooperative

A worker- or member-owned enterprise.

copolymer

A *polymer made of two or more different types of *monomers.

coppicing

A form of management in which woody plants are repeatedly cut near the ground so that they resprout.

COP21

The 21st Conference of the Parties to the UN Framework Convention on Climate Change who negotiated and signed the 2015 *Paris Agreement.

coral

Tiny marine animals who build reefs of calcium carbonate and derive energy from symbiotic algae.

coral bleaching

A die-off that occurs when symbiotic algae disappear from coral reefs so that the *corals lose their food source and their color.

core

The central part of planet Earth, lying beneath the *mantle and composed of iron and nickel.

core habitat *See* interior habitat.

cornucopianism

The belief that human ingenuity and technology will continue to support economic growth and overcome any environmental constraints.

Corporate Average Fuel Economy (CAFE)

Fuel efficiency standards for cars and light trucks that must be achieved by each automaker in the US, increasing each year.

corporate social responsibility (CSR)

The voluntary commitment of a business to take responsibility for the social, economic, and environmental impacts of its activities.

corporation

A legal entity that is required by law to make decisions which financially benefit its stockholders. *Compare* benefit corporation.

correlation

A relationship between variables; not necessarily causal.

corridor

A linear landscape element that connects otherwise isolated *habitat patches, allowing movement and dispersal. *See also* matrix; patch.

corrosive

A chemical agent able to deteriorate materials.

cosmology

The study of the history and structure of the universe.

cost-benefit analysis

A comparison, usually financial, of the negative and positive impacts of a given action.

cost effectiveness
The extent to which a particular outcome can be achieved at the lowest cost possible.

coupling
The links between any two components of a system. *See also* decoupling.

courtyard
An exterior space surrounded by building walls and open to the sky.

cover crop
A temporary plant cover that prevents erosion and adds nutrients to the soil. *See also* green manure.

cp *See* candlepower.

CPR *See* common pool resource.

CPTED *See* crime prevention through environmental design.

cracking
One of several chemical processes that break down *polymers into other *hydrocarbon products.

cradle to cradle
A design approach in which materials are thought of as nutrients which recycle continuously.

cradle to gate
The scope of a product life cycle that extends from raw material acquisition through final manufacturing but excludes product use and disposal.

cradle to grave
The scope of a product life cycle that extends from raw material acquisition through product use and disposal, but excludes recycling or reuse.

crime prevention through environmental design (CPTED)
A design approach for discouraging crime and promoting safety through reducing crime opportunities and promoting positive social behavior.

criteria
Plural form of criterion; the specific values or conditions that must be met in order to meet a standard or to be awarded *certification.

criteria pollutants
Major air pollutants regulated by the US Clean Air Act: *particulates, *carbon monoxide, sulfur oxides, *nitrogen oxides, *lead, and ground-level *ozone.

critical path method
A planning and scheduling tool which calculates the shortest time needed and shows the activities that are most important in order to complete a project on schedule.

critical root zone
The area around a tree within which soil must be protected from excavation or compaction; also known as the tree protection zone.

critical slowing down
An early warning signal of an approaching *tipping point or critical transition to a new state in a complex system consisting of an increase in recovery time following small *disturbances.

critical thinking
The intellectually disciplined process of analyzing, synthesizing, and evaluating information using observation, logic, and reasoning skills.

critical transition *See* tipping point.

crop residue
Organic residue remaining after the harvesting and processing of a crop.

crop rotation
The practice of alternating the type of crop grown in a particular field each season.

cross-cutting issue
An issue that cannot be adequately understood without reference to the interactions of several dimensions that are usually treated separately for policy purposes.

cross-scale
Referring to processes at one spatial or temporal scale interacting with processes at another scale.

cross ventilation
A method of using natural ventilation for cooling that uses wind pressure to allow air to flow across a space.

crude oil
*Petroleum as it exists in underground reservoirs or after extraction and before refining.

crust
The thin, outer layer of the *lithosphere that contacts the *atmosphere, *hydrosphere, and *biota and lies above the *mantle.

cryosphere
Earth's ice and snow cover.

CSA See community-supported agriculture.

CSP See concentrating solar power.

CSR See corporate social responsibility.

cullet
Crushed glass.

cultural ecosystem services
The non-material benefits people obtain from *ecosystems, including spiritual enrichment, cognitive development, recreation, and aesthetic experience.

cultural hazard
A human health *hazard resulting from where one lives, socioeconomic status,

occupation, and behavioral choices. Also known as social hazard.

cultural resource
A site, structure, landscape, or object that provides evidence of past human activity, or a natural feature significant to a group of people traditionally associated with it.

culture
The systems of knowledge, beliefs, and behavior patterns shared by a group of people and passed from one generation to the next.

culvert
Any structure, not classified as a bridge, that allows water to flow under a road or path.

curbside collection
A program in which recyclable materials are collected at the curb for transfer to collection sites or processing facilities. *Compare* drop-off collection.

curing
The conversion of raw products to finished material, as in the cooling of a thermoplastic into a solid product or allowing concrete to harden to the required strength by maintaining appropriate humidity and temperature for a specified time.

current, electric
The rate of flow of *electrons, measured in amperes.

cut and fill
A method of grading in which material is cut from a higher ground surface and the excavated material is used for fill to raise the surface of a lower area.

cut bank
An *erosion feature found along the outside of a stream bend.

Cuyahoga River

A US river in Ohio whose polluted surface caught fire in 1952 and 1969.

cyanobacteria

Photosynthetic bacteria. Formerly known as blue-green algae.

cyclone

A rotational storm originating over oceans. *See also* hurricane; typhoon; tornado.

D

dam

A barrier built across a river to control flow or to create a reservoir. *See also* hydroelectric dam.

data

A collection of pieces of quantitative information; plural form of datum, a single piece of information.

daylight factor

The ratio of daylight *illuminance inside a structure to the illuminance outside the structure under totally overcast sky conditions.

daylighting

1 (buildings) The use of natural sunlight for illumination in order to reduce or eliminate electric lighting. Daylighting strategies use *toplighting, *sidelighting, *light shelves, *clerestory windows, or a combination.

2 (stream restoration) The act of returning a diverted or buried stream to the surface so that it flows in an open waterway aboveground.

dB *See* decibel.

deadhead trip

A trip in which a truck or tractor-trailer travels empty, without a load.

dead zone

An area of extremely low oxygen *concentration in an ocean or lake leading to deaths of aquatic organisms, caused by *eutrophication.

decarbonization

The process of shifting from high-carbon energy sources to less carbon-intensive fuels.

decibel (dB)

A unit of measure for sound power based on the pressure produced in air by a noise.

deciduous

A plant that loses its leaves seasonally. *Compare* evergreen.

decommissioning

The activities necessary to take a facility out of service and dispose of its components after its useful life.

decomposer

A *fungus or *bacterium that breaks down organic material into simpler component elements.

decomposition

The breaking down of matter by *fungi and *bacteria into smaller or simpler components.

deconstruction
The process of selectively removing and salvaging building materials for reuse.

decoupling
The condition in which *development occurs without increases in environmental impact.

deductive reasoning
Logical reasoning from general to specific. *Compare* inductive reasoning.

deep ecology
A philosophy that nature has *intrinsic value and a right to flourish, and that humans have an obligation to organize their societies accordingly.

deep injection well *See* injection well.

deep time
The multimillion-year scale of geologic time.

deforestation
The removal of all trees and conversion of forested land to non-forest. *Compare* afforestation; reforestation; *see also* land use.

degradation
1 The decomposition of a compound through the breaking of molecular bonds.
2 The downcutting of a stream channel through erosion.
3 A lessening of *ecosystem function.

degree day *See* heating degree day; cooling degree day.

de-listing
The removal of a formerly *endangered species from the list of endangered species. *Compare* listing.

Delphi
A structured group communication method which uses multiple rounds of questionnaires and responses to facilitate consensus.

demand
1 (economics) The quantity of a product *consumers will buy at a particular price. *Compare* supply.
2 (energy) The rate at which power is used.

demand side management
Programs to modify *consumer demands for energy, including energy efficiency and shifting of demand to nonpeak hours.

demand-type water heater *See* tankless water heater.

dematerialization
A reduction in the use of materials needed to produce a product or service.

demographic bonus
A one-time benefit for *populations that pass through a *demographic transition in which the proportion of children and older adults relative to the number of working adults decreases.

demographic transition
The shift from high birth rates and death rates to low birth rates and death rates in developed countries.

demography
A field of social science that applies the principles of *population ecology to human populations.

denitrification
The process by which *bacteria convert nitrates to gaseous nitrogen and nitrous oxide. *Compare* nitrogen fixation.

dense non-aqueous phase liquid (DNAPL)
A *non-aqueous phase liquid with a specific gravity greater than 1.0 that sinks to the bottom of an *aquifer.

density
The number of people or *dwelling units per acre.

depolymerization
Chemical processes that break down polymers into monomers. *See also* chemical recycling.

deposition
The settling of eroded soil particles at a new location.

desalination
The removal of dissolved salt from seawater. Also known as desalinization.

desert
A *biome with less than 10 inches of precipitation per year.

desertification
The conversion of formerly productive land to *desert.

design for deconstruction
The design of buildings to enable building materials to be recovered and reused following renovation or demolition.

design for disassembly
Design that allows future recovery and reuse of components and materials in a product.

design for environment
The practice of designing products and manufacturing processes in environmentally responsible ways.

design storm
A rainstorm of a given intensity and frequency of recurrence used as the basis for calculating sizes of stormwater facilities.

detection
(climate science) The process of determining the presence and magnitude of changes to a system. *Compare* attribution.

detention basin
A pond or depression for temporarily storing *stormwater runoff to allow pollutants to settle out and to reduce the peak rate of flow. *See also* retention basin.

developed country
A nation with high average per capita income and level of industrialization relative to less developed countries. *Compare* developing country.

developing country
A nation with low average per capita income and level of industrialization relative to more developed countries. *Compare* developed country.

development
An increase in the quality of goods and services, with or without quantitative growth; development is a qualitative measure.

dew point
The temperature at which *condensation begins at a given atmospheric moisture content.

diatomic
A molecule composed of two atoms.

diatoms
Algae with cell walls made of silica, found in almost every aquatic environment.

diesel
A heavy petroleum distillate used as fuel.

diffusion of innovation
The process in which an innovative idea or behavior spreads through social contacts. Also known as social diffusion.

digester
A tank in which *anaerobic bacteria break down organic matter.

digestion
The *biochemical decomposition of organic matter. *See also* aerobic digestion; anaerobic digestion.

digital terrain mapping
The representation of a portion of the Earth's surface stored in a digital file containing regularly spaced point locations with an elevation attribute.

dike
A wall or barrier to prevent uncontrolled flooding or to prevent a *contaminant spill from spreading.

dimethyl sulphide (DMS)
A sulfur gas emitted by marine *algae as a waste product which facilitates cloud formation.

dioxins
A family of *toxic chlorinated chemical compounds formed as products of *combustion and industrial processes.

direct current (DC)
Electric *current in which *electrons flow in one direction only. *Compare* alternating current.

discharge rate
The volume of water flow in a channel or from a site during a given time; commonly expressed as cubic feet per second.

discounting
A practice in economics in which future costs and future benefits are calculated to be less valuable than present ones.

dish concentrator
*Concentrating solar technology in which a single parabolic mirror focuses sunlight on a single point; typically drives a *Stirling engine.

disincentive
An economic or material penalty in return for acting in a particular way which is harmful to a set goal. *Compare* incentive.

disinfectant
A chemical or physical process that kills microorganisms.

dispersion
The spreading of matter from the center of a *contaminant mass.

disposable
Materials or products designed to be used once and then discarded. *Compare* durable goods.

dissolution
The *transport of a *contaminant by the transfer of its molecules to water; the process of dissolving.

dissolved oxygen (DO)
The amount of oxygen in water freely available to aquatic life; usually expressed in *ppm.

distillate fuel oil
A general classification for the *petroleum fractions produced in conventional distillation operations; includes fuel oils and some *diesels.

distillation
1 (water treatment) The process of boiling water to produce steam, which is then captured by condensing the water vapor, in order to remove salt or other *contaminants.
2 (pollution treatment) The use of heat to separate water from more volatile substances.

distillation effect *See* grasshopper effect.

distributed generation
The generation of power by small power plants located close to where it is used. *See also* microgrid; smart grid.

distributed power
Power produced by small, independent power sources, used near where it is produced. *Compare* centralized power.

distributive governance
Networked *governance that distributes decision-making to the level where it is handled most effectively.

district heating
A system that uses a central source of heat which is distributed through pipes to a group of buildings.

disturbance
A natural or human-caused event such as fire, flood, or urban development that changes the structure and function of an *ecosystem.

disturbance regime
The spatial pattern, scale, frequency, and intensity of *disturbances in a given area over time.

diurnal
1 A process that has a daily cycle.
2 An organism active during the daytime.

diversion hydroelectric *See* run-of-river.

diversion rate
The percentage of material diverted for *recycling, *composting, or *reuse, compared to the total quantity of *waste.

diversity
The range of variation or differences among components in a system, including the number of different types, the number of members of each type, and the degree of difference between the types.

diversity, genetic *See* genetic diversity.

divestment
The process of selling off subsidiary business interests or investments that are considered unethical.

DMS *See* dimethyl sulphide.

DNAPL *See* dense non-aqueous phase liquid.

DO *See* dissolved oxygen.

domain
One of three primary divisions of life as determined by RNA sequencing. *See* *Archaea; *bacteria; *eukaryote.

domestic water
Water used by fixtures such as toilets, showerheads, and faucets and appliances such as clothes washers and dishwashers.

dominant paradigm
The current development *paradigm which emphasizes industrialization, centralized planning, and *economic growth.

dose
The quantity of a substance to which an organism is exposed.

downcycling
A characteristic of reprocessing a material in which the quality of the material decreases over time.

downwelling
In the ocean, the sinking of surface water toward the ocean floor. *Compare* upwelling.

drainage basin *See* watershed.

drainage divide
A ridge or topographic high point between adjacent watersheds.

drainageway
General term for an aboveground route along which water moves.

drainfield
In a *septic system, the network of pipes through which *wastewater is dispersed into the soil.

drain inlet
A drainage-system receptacle which does not contain a sump and which directs *surface runoff directly to a drain pipe.

drawdown cone *See* cone of depression.

drift net
A vertical fishing net that drifts in water, catching everything in its path.

drilling fluid
A synthetic-base or water-base fluid used in oil and gas extraction to lubricate drill bits, remove cuttings, control pressure, or force crude oil to the surface. *Compare* produced water.

drilling mud *See* drilling fluid.

drip irrigation
A low-pressure system in which water drips from perforated tubes or small emitters placed near plants.

driver
A force or condition that influences and causes a system to change.

drop-off collection
A method in which individuals transport recyclable materials to designated collection sites. *Compare* curbside collection.

drought
A period of abnormally dry weather long enough to cause serious water shortages for humans and *ecosystems.

dry cooling system
In a *thermoelectric power plant, a system that circulates water between a steam condenser and a dry condenser located outdoors, cooled by fans. Also known as a dry closed-loop cooling system. *Compare* closed-loop cooling system.

dry farming
Growing crops without the use of irrigation.

dryland
An *ecosystem characterized by lack of water; includes cultivated lands, scrublands, *shrublands, *grasslands, *savannas, semi-deserts, and true *deserts.

dual-fuel vehicle
1   A *bi-fuel vehicle.
2   A vehicle which runs on *natural gas and uses diesel for ignition assistance.

duff
A layer of forest *litter and other organic debris on top of the soil.

dump
A place where *waste is deposited without further treatment or protection.

dumpster
A front-load, lidded metal trash receptacle designed to be dumped by a specialized truck. *See also* roll-off bin.

dune
A mound or ridge of *sand formed by *wind.

durable goods
Products with a useful life measured in years and that are replaced infrequently. *Compare* disposable.

Dust Bowl
An event triggered by *drought in the 1930s when areas of the US Great

Plains lost large amounts of *topsoil due to wind *erosion.

dwelling unit
A separate living space including kitchen intended for occupancy by an individual or family-size group.

dynamic equilibrium
The condition in which the amount of energy entering a system equals the energy leaving the system and the system's dynamic processes lead to a steady state.

E

E10

A fuel mixture of 10% *ethanol and 90% gasoline. Sometimes known as gasohol.

E85

A fuel mixture of 85% *ethanol and 15% gasoline.

E95

A fuel mixture of 95% *ethanol and 5% gasoline.

Earth Charter

An international declaration of fundamental values and principles for building a just, sustainable, and peaceful global society, launched as a UN initiative and completed as a global civil-society initiative in 2000.

Earth Day

An annual international event focused on environmental issues.

Earthrise

A 1968 photograph of Earth rising over the moon's horizon taken from the Apollo 8 rocket.

earth-sheltered design

A method in which buildings are constructed partially or totally below ground.

Earth Summit, Rio

The UN Conference on Environment and Development held in Rio de Janeiro in 1992.

Earth Summit 2002

The UN World Summit on Sustainable Development held in Johannesburg, South Africa, in 2002.

Earth system

The total complex of atmosphere, hydrosphere, lithosphere, and biosphere that influence conditions at the Earth's surface.

Earth system science

The study of the Earth as an integrated *system including the interactions of the *atmosphere, *hydrosphere, *lithosphere, and *biosphere.

earth tube

A large diameter, long tube buried underground that uses the *thermal mass of the earth as part of a *natural ventilation system. *See also* geothermal heating and cooling; ground source heat pump.

easement

A right of way or right to use a piece of land owned by another person.

EBM *See* energy balance model.

eccentricity
The change of shape of the Earth's elliptical orbit on cycles of 10,000 and 400,000 years. *See also* Milankovitch cycles.

ecoagriculture *See* agroecology.

ecobabble
Speech which uses the technical language of *ecology to make the user appear ecologically aware.

eco-cemetery
A cemetery which protects sensitive habitats, allows only nontoxic and *biodegradable burial materials, and prohibits the use of embalming fluids and *heavy metals.

ecocentrism *See* biocentrism.

ecocity
A city modeled on the self-sustaining resilient structure and function of natural *ecosystems and built on principles of ecological integrity and social equity.

eco-district
A collaborative planning approach that focuses on regenerative urban development at the neighborhood scale, linking *green buildings, *smart infrastructure, and behavior.

ecoduct
Term for a *wildlife overpass, more commonly used in European countries.

eco-effectiveness
A central strategy in *cradle-to-cradle design centered around *closed-loop cycles. *Compare* eco-efficiency.

eco-efficiency
An approach to product and process design that seeks to minimize material consumption, waste, and pollution. *Compare* eco-effectiveness.

ecofeminism
The concept that historic oppression of women and exploitation of nature are linked.

eco-industrial park
A complex of industrial facilities which applies the principles of *industrial ecology in an *industrial ecosystem.

eco-innovation
General term for innovations in business that minimize environmental impacts, use natural resources responsibly, and incorporate life cycle thinking.

eco-label
A label which gives information about a product or service in terms of its environmental or social impacts.

ecolinguistics
A subdiscipline of linguistics which studies the role of language in environmental problems and solutions.

ecological design
General term for ecologically responsible design modeled on natural systems.

ecological economics
A discipline that merges *economics and *ecology and conceives of the economy as a subsystem of the Earth *ecosystem. *Compare* environmental economics; neoclassical economics.

Ecological Footprint
A measure of the demand a person, *population, or activity places on nature in order to produce the resources it consumes and to absorb the waste it generates, usually expressed as acres or hectares of productive land and water. *See also* carrying capacity; global hectare.

ecological infrastructure
An area which provides *ecosystem services to a community or city. *See also* green infrastructure.

ecological integrity *See* integrity, ecological.

ecological justice
The recognition that all living beings and ecological systems have value and the right to thrive independent of their usefulness to humans. *Environmental justice is justice for humans; ecological justice is justice for other beings and ecological systems.

ecological literacy
A fundamental understanding of ecological principles including an understanding of systems. Also known as ecoliteracy; often used interchangeably with *environmental literacy.

ecological restoration *See* restoration.

ecological risk assessment
The process for evaluating the risk of adverse environmental impacts as a result of human impacts such as *chemicals, land use change, and *climate change. Known as *environmental risk assessment in Europe.

ecological rucksack
The total weight of material "carried" by a product; the material displaced in order to extract, process, and use the material over the course of its lifetime.

ecological succession *See* succession.

ecology
The study of the relationships between organisms and their environment.

ecology, four laws of *See* four laws of ecology

Eco-Management and Audit Scheme (EMAS)
A sustainability management and reporting standard developed by the European Commission and used by *organizations throughout Europe.

economic growth
An increase in economic activity over a period of time, measured by *gross domestic product.

economics
The study of the allocation of resources for the production, distribution, and consumption of goods and services. *See also* classical economics; neoclassical economics; environmental economics; ecological economics.

economies of scale
A decrease in the cost of producing each unit as the volume of production increases.

economizer
An *HVAC cycle that draws in cool outside air to minimize the use of mechanical cooling.

economy
The system of production, distribution, and consumption of goods and services.

ecoregion
A physical area with a particular combination of environmental conditions, including *climate, *topography, geology, and *vegetation.

ecosystem
A system of living organisms interacting with each other and their physical environment.

ecosystem function
The processes resulting from interacting elements of an ecosystem including *structure, *biodiversity, and *biogeochemical cycles.

ecosystem health
The state of an ecosystem in which the attributes of *biodiversity are expressed

within normal ranges, relative to its ecological stage of development.

ecosystem services
The essential benefits people obtain from ecosystem processes. *See also* provisioning services; regulating services.

ecotax *See* green tax.

ecotone
A transitional zone between two *ecosystems.

ecotourism
Responsible travel to natural areas that conserves the *environment and sustains the *well-being of local people; often includes interpretation and education.

ecovillage
A community modeled on the self-sustaining resilient structure and function of natural ecosystems and built on principles of ecological integrity and social equity.

edge effect
Altered environmental conditions that impact organisms living near the edge of a *fragmented habitat.

edible forest *See* food forest.

edible landscape
A designed landscape that uses food plants as design materials for aesthetic value as well as consumption.

edible wall
A *green wall on which food plants are grown.

EEA *See* European Environment Agency.

efficiency
The proportion of output per unit of input.

effluent
Wastewater that flows from a process, treatment system, or power plant.

EIA *See* Energy Information Administration; environmental impact assessment.

EIS *See* environmental impact statement.

electrical charge
The property of matter in which an object has more or fewer *electrons than *protons.

electrical energy
A form of *energy characterized by the movement of *electrical charge.

electrical equipment
Any machine powered by *electricity, such as major appliances and power tools. *Compare* electronic equipment.

electric current *See* current.

electric hybrid vehicle *See* electric vehicle; hybrid electric vehicle.

electricity *See* electrical energy.

electric meter
A device for measuring the *electric power delivered to a *utility customer; *see also* kilowatt-hours.

electric power
The rate at which electric energy is transferred; *see also* watt; megawatt.

electric power grid *See* grid.

electric vehicle (EV)
A motor vehicle driven by an electric motor that draws *current from batteries, *fuel cells, *photovoltaic arrays, or other sources of electric *current. *Compare* hybrid vehicle. *See also* battery-electric vehicle.

electrolysis
A process of separating a liquid into chemical parts by passing electric *current through it; used to produce *hydrogen for *fuel cells.

electromagnetic energy
A form of *energy that travels in waves.

electron
A negatively charged particle that surrounds the nucleus of an *atom.

electronic equipment
Equipment operated by *semiconductor devices, such as computers, cellphones, and television sets.

electronic waste (e-waste)
Discarded electrical or electronic equipment.

electrostatic precipitator
A device for removing *particulate matter from *flue gas by inducing an electrostatic charge and collecting the particles on oppositely charged plates.

element
A substance made from a single type of *atom which cannot be broken down into other substances. *Compare* compound.

elevation
Vertical distance relative to a given datum, such as sea level.

elevator speech
A concise summary, brief enough to be conveyed within a 30-second elevator trip.

El Niño
A strong warming of surface water in the eastern Pacific Ocean that occurs every 2 to 10 years causing a major shift in oceanic and atmospheric circulation. *Compare* La Niña. *See also* El Niño/ Southern Oscillation.

El Niño/Southern Oscillation (ENSO)
An irregular climate oscillation in the Pacific Ocean involving large-scale changes in ocean surface temperatures and winds; gives rise to *El Niño and *La Niña conditions. *See also* North Atlantic Oscillation.

EMAS *See* Eco-Management and Audit Scheme.

embodied energy
The total *energy used to produce, transport, and dispose of a product.

emergence
The spontaneous appearance of novel properties at the level of a *system that cannot be predicted by knowledge of the system's parts.

emergent vegetation
Plants which are rooted in shallow water with leaves at or above the water surface. *See also* marsh.

emergy
The amount of *energy used in transformations directly or indirectly to make a product or service; can be a shortened form of *embodied energy or of "energy memory."

emission factor
The rate of *emission per unit of activity, output, or input.

emissions
The release of gases into the *atmosphere.

emissions trading
The buying and selling of permits to pollute; also known as cap and trade.

emissivity
The relative capacity of a surface to emit heat by radiation. *See also* low-emissivity coating.

emittance
The ability of a material to radiate absorbed *heat, expressed on a scale of 0 to 1 or 0% to 100%.

emitter
1 (drip irrigation) A device which releases water at a slow rate.
2 (electronics) A region in a transistor.

emjoule
The measurement unit for *emergy.

empirical
Based on observation of physical phenomena.

EMS *See* environmental management system.

encapsulation
A method of treating hazardous waste by covering it with an inert material to prevent its release.

endangered species
A *species considered to be facing a high risk of *extinction in the wild in the near future.

Endangered Species Act (ESA)
US law giving legal protection to *endangered species and their *habitats. *See also* listing; de-listing.

endemic
Native to and found only in a particular geographic area.

endocrine disruptor
A pollutant that interferes with normal hormone functions.

end-of-pipe
Technologies that are applied after environmental impacts have occurred.

energy
The ability to do work. Energy can change form and can appear as *mechanical, *chemical, *nuclear, *electrical, *light, or *heat energy.

energy audit
A systematic, detailed analysis of how and where a building uses *energy.

energy balance
The difference between the total incoming and total outgoing *energy; a *system is in energy balance when it loses as much energy as it gains.

energy balance model (EBM)
A simple global *climate model that computes *energy balance but omits other elements of the *climate system.

energy budget
An accounting of all the *energy flowing into and out of a *system.

energy carrier
A substance that contains *energy which can later be converted to another form of energy.

energy conservation
Reduction or elimination of unnecessary energy use. *See also* energy efficiency.

energy density
The amount of *energy per volume or mass.

energy efficiency
Using less energy to perform the same tasks.

Energy Information Administration (EIA)
An agency within the US Department of Energy charged by Congress with providing energy data, analysis, and projections. *See also* International Energy Agency.

energy intensity
The ratio of energy input to economic or physical output.

energy management system
A control system capable of monitoring environmental and system loads and adjusting *HVAC output in order to conserve energy while maintaining comfort.

energy poverty
Lack of access to modern *energy services including *electricity and clean cooking facilities.

energy quality
The ability of a form of *energy to do useful *work.

energy recovery ventilation (ERV)
The process of transferring the heat or coolness in air exhausted from a building to the outside air being pulled into the building.

energy returned on energy invested (EROEI)
The difference between the *energy used to produce a *fuel and the energy contained in the final product.

energy security
The uninterrupted availability of *energy sources at an affordable price.

energy servant
A quantity of *energy equivalent to the amount of power a standard human could produce, about one *kilowatt-hour per day per energy servant.

energy service
The amount of useful work done by each unit of *fuel.

energy services company (ESCO)
A company which provides *measurement and verification and *energy efficiency services for a building and whose fees are paid for out of the energy savings.

energy utilization index (EUI)
An index used to measure building efficiency, usually expressed as a ratio of *Btu per square foot of gross floor area per year.

energy vampire *See* phantom power.

engineered lumber
A building material made of wood fibers held together by a *resin binder.

enhanced greenhouse effect
The concept that the natural *greenhouse effect has been enhanced by *anthropogenic *emissions of *greenhouse gases.

enhanced oil recovery *See* oil recovery.

ENSO *See* El Niño/Southern Oscillation.

enteric fermentation
A digestive process in ruminant animals in which *anaerobic bacteria *decompose food and emit *methane.

enthalpy
The sum of sensible heat and latent heat present in air.

entropy
The degree of disorder in a *system.

entropy, law of *See* thermodynamics, second law.

envelope
The elements of a building that enclose internal space, including walls, windows, roof, floor, and foundation.

environment
All the living and nonliving external conditions that affect and interact with organisms, *populations, or other living *systems.

environmental economics

The branch of *neoclassical economics that addresses environmental issues using traditional economic mechanisms. Compare ecological economics.

environmental education

A process in which individuals investigate their *environment and learn to make intelligent and informed decisions about caring for it.

environmental ethics

The branch of philosophy that studies the moral value of, and humans' ethical relationship to, the nonhuman world.

environmental health

The discipline which studies the effects of environmental factors on human health.

environmental history

The study of human relationships to the natural world through time.

environmental impact assessment (EIA)

The formal process of identifying and evaluating the environmental consequences of an actual or proposed action.

environmentalism

A philosophy and social movement focused on protecting the *natural *environment.

environmental justice

The concept that access to a clean, healthy *environment is a fundamental human right. Compare ecological justice.

environmental literacy

A fundamental understanding of ecological principles and the systems of the *biosphere, together with the knowledge and motivations to work toward solutions of current environmental problems

and the prevention of new ones. See also ecological literacy.

environmentally preferable

Products or services that have a lesser or reduced negative effect on human health and the *environment when compared with competing products or services that serve the same purpose.

environmentally preferable purchasing (EPP)

The procurement of products or services whose environmental impacts have been found to be less damaging to the *environment and human health when compared to competing products/services. Also known as *green purchasing.

environmental management system (EMS)

A formal system within an *organization for developing, implementing, and maintaining environmental policies and procedures. See also management system.

environmental policy

*Public policy concerning environmental issues including *pollution and protection of natural systems.

Environmental Protection Agency (EPA)

A US agency responsible for implementing and enforcing environmental laws and for educating the public.

environmental racism

The disproportionate impact of environmental *hazards on minority communities.

environmental risk assessment

The process for evaluating the risk of adverse environmental impacts as a result of human impacts such as *chemicals, land use change, and climate change. Known as *ecological risk assessment in the US.

environmental science
The scientific study of the *biosphere and human interactions with it.

environmental studies
An interdisciplinary field of study that incorporates the sciences, social sciences, humanities, policy, and planning.

environmental tax See green tax.

environmental toxicology
The study of the effects and risks of *toxicants on the *environment, wildlife, and human health.

E&P
Exploration and production.

EPA See Environmental Protection Agency.

ephemeral
Temporary or short-lived, such as spring wildflowers or *vernal pools.

ephemeral stream
A stream without *baseflow; one that flows only during or after rainstorms or snowmelt events. Compare intermittent stream; perennial stream.

epidemiology
The study of the causes and effects of disease and its distribution in human *populations.

epistemology
(philosophy) Theory of knowledge; the study of knowledge and justified belief.

epoch
A subdivision of the *geologic time scale. See also Anthropocene epoch; Holocene epoch.

EPP See environmentally preferable purchasing.

EPS See expanded polystyrene.

equilibrium
The state of a *system in which opposing influences are balanced and in which the system will remain unless disturbed. See also dynamic equilibrium; static equilibrium.

equity
Fairness of rights, distribution, and access; can refer to resources, services, or power depending on context. See also environmental justice; social justice.

EROEI See energy returned on energy invested.

erosion
A process in which rock or soil is loosened, removed, and transported from one place to another by the action of water, wind, or other natural agents.

ERV See energy recovery ventilation.

ESA See Endangered Species Act.

ESCO See energy services company.

espalier
The practice of pruning and training fruit trees to grow flat against a wall or trellis as a way to conserve space in confined areas.

estuary
An area where the *fresh water of a river mixes with salt water from the ocean.

ethanol
Ethyl alcohol produced from *biomass. See also biofuel.

ethics
(philosophy) The study of right and wrong; the study of moral beliefs and conduct. See also environmental ethics.

ethnoecology
The study of the various forms of traditional environmental knowledge in groups of *indigenous people. *See also* traditional ecological knowledge.

EUI *See* energy utilization index.

eukaryote
Single- and multi-celled organisms made from cells containing nuclei; one of the three primary *domains of life. *Compare* prokaryote. *See also* Archaea; bacteria.

European Environment Agency (EEA)
The agency of the European Union responsible for providing reliable information on the *environment to policymakers and the public.

European Green Belt
A large-scale *habitat *corridor and ecological network connecting multiple nations in Europe and Russia.

eutrophication
Accelerated plant growth and decay in aquatic environments caused by nitrogen and phosphorus pollution and resulting in oxygen depletion.

EV *See* electric vehicle.

evacuated tube collector
A type of *solar water heater consisting of glass tubes with a vacuum inside and containing a heat-transfer fluid.

evaporation
The process by which a liquid is converted to a gas.

evaporative cooler
A device that uses the *latent heat of evaporation to absorb *sensible heat from outdoor air passed over moist pads and circulated by a fan. Also known as a swamp cooler.

evaporative cooling tower *See* cooling tower.

evaporative emissions
Emissions from fuel which *evaporates from vehicle *fuel systems or during refueling.

evaporator
The *heat exchanger in a *heat pump or other refrigeration cycle that absorbs heat from refrigerant. *See also* condenser.

evapotranspiration
The combined effect of *evaporation from soil and water and *transpiration by plants.

evergreen
A plant whose leaves or needles remain on the plant all year. *Compare* deciduous.

evidence-based design
An approach to designing the built *environment in which decisions are based on the best available current research evidence.

evolution
1 A process of continuous change to a more *complex or better state.
2 A genetically based change in the heritable traits of a *population of organisms over successive generations.

e-waste *See* electronic waste.

exergy
(thermodynamics) A measure of available useful *energy.

exotic species
A species that originated in another region than the one in which it now occurs.

expanded polystyrene (EPS)
A product made from *polystyrene beads that have been expanded and packed to form a closed-cell foam; used for building insulation, packing material, and foam containers.

experiential learning
Education which involves learning by doing.

exploration and production (E&P) waste
Waste generated by oil and gas drilling.

exponential growth
An increase in quantity by a fixed percentage over time.

exposure
The contact of an organism with a substance.

ex situ
A location off-site or removed from the original location. *Compare in situ.*

extended producer responsibility
Financial incentives and legal requirements to promote the integration of environmental costs associated with goods throughout their *life cycles into the market price of the products.

extensive green roof
A roof planted with a growing medium at a depth of 6 inches or less.

externality
A cost which is external to the entity creating the damage and not reflected in the price.

extinction
The death of all individuals within a species. *See also* background extinction; mass extinction.

extinction vortex
The process in which mutually reinforcing *extinction forces cause a declining *population to move faster toward extinction.

extirpation
The disappearance of a local *population of a species that still exists elsewhere. Also known as local extinction.

extraction
The process by which *petroleum and *natural gas are removed from wells, including exploration and production.

extremophile
An organism with the ability to thrive in conditions considered extreme to humans, including high temperature, high pressure, or the absence of oxygen or light.

eyes on the street
Informal term for natural surveillance of streets and public spaces. *See also* crime prevention through environmental design.

F

facilitator
A neutral third party trained in effective group facilitation methods whose task is to guide group processes.

Factor 4
A concept which proposes that humans should reduce their consumption of resources to one-fourth of the current levels in order not to exceed the planet's *carrying capacity.

Factor 10
A concept which proposes that humans should reduce their consumption of resources to one-tenth of the current levels in order not to exceed the planet's *carrying capacity.

factory farm *See* concentrated animal feeding operation.

failed state
A state, or self-governing political body, in which the ability to govern has broken down.

faint young sun paradox
The apparent discrepancy between the fact that the sun was 30% less luminous 3.8 billion years ago so that Earth's

surface should have been frozen, and the evidence of liquid water and microbial life during the same time period.

Fair Trade
A trading system, verified by *certification, in which products meet international standards for fair prices, fair labor conditions, and environmental *sustainability.

FAO *See* Food and Agriculture Organization.

FAR *See* floor area ratio.

farmers' market
A public venue where multiple farmers sell their produce directly to *consumers.

fascine *See* wattle.

fate
The description of how a *pollutant changes over time.

FCV *See* fuel-cell vehicle.

fecal coliform bacteria
A group of *bacteria found in the feces of humans and other animals which are used as indicators of disease-causing bacteria.

fecundity
The capacity of an organism or *pop-
ulation to produce viable offspring.
Compare fertility.

feebate
A system that taxes socially undesirable activities and products and uses
the money to support more desirable
ones; a recently coined word combining "fee" and "rebate."

feedback
A circular mechanism in which the
result of an initial process triggers
changes in a second process that in turn
influences the initial process.

feedback, negative
A feedback interaction which decreases
the original change.

feedback, positive
A feedback interaction which increases
or amplifies the original change.

feed-in tariff
A price above market rates that a *utility
must pay to small, non-utility energy producers for *energy they supply back to the
grid, if mandated by government *policy.

feedlot *See* concentrated animal feeding operation.

feedstock
The raw material that is required for
some industrial process.

fen
A type of *wetland that accumulates
*peat deposits, generally remains wet,
and supports *marsh *vegetation.

fencerow *See* hedgerow.

fenestration
A light-transmitting opening in a wall
or roof.

Ferrel cell
A large-scale circulation of air through
the entire depth of the *troposphere
in the mid-latitudes, with air flowing
poleward near the surface and toward
the equator at higher altitudes. *Compare*
Hadley cell; polar cell.

ferrous metal
Magnetic metal derived from iron.

fertility
The capacity to produce offspring. *See
also* fertility rate. *Compare* fecundity.

fertility rate
The number of children born per woman
during her lifetime. *See also* replacement
fertility rate.

fertilization, carbon dioxide *See*
carbon dioxide fertilization.

fertilizer
A substance that adds inorganic or
organic plant nutrients to soil to
improve its ability to grow crops or
other *vegetation. *See also* fertilizer,
synthetic; organic fertilizer.

fertilizer, organic *See* organic fertilizer.

fertilizer, synthetic
Commercially prepared mixtures of
plant nutrients such as nitrates, phosphates, and potassium applied to the
soil to increase crop yields. *Compare*
organic fertilizer.

fifth great turning *See* Great Transition.

fill
Human-made deposits of soil, rock,
and/or waste material.

filter strip
A vegetated *buffer zone used for
removing *sediments and *pollutants
from *runoff and *wastewater.

filtration
The removal of *pollutants such as *sediment as water passes through a soil, organic, and/or fabric medium.

finished water
Water that has passed through all the processes in a water treatment plant and is ready to be delivered to *consumers.

finishing
(wastewater treatment) *See* tertiary treatment.

first flush
The initial quantity of water that runs off a surface at the beginning of a rainstorm.

first-party certification
A self-declaration by an *organization itself. *Compare* certification; third-party certification.

Fischer-Tropsch process
A process for making liquid *fuel from *fossil fuels or *biomass.

fishery
1 A particular *species of targeted fish.
2 A particular marine area being fished commercially.

fission
The splitting apart of heavy nuclei to release some of the *energy that was binding the atomic particles together. *See also* nuclear energy. *Compare* fusion.

fixture
1 A device to deliver or drain water, such as toilets, showerheads, and faucets.
2 A complete lighting unit. Also known as a *luminaire.

flagship species
A large, charismatic animal *species that can generate public support for *conservation efforts.

flaring
The pressure-relief process of venting and burning *natural gas through smokestacks at oil and gas wells and refineries.

flat plate collector
A type of *solar water heater consisting of a thin, rectangular box, a dark-colored absorber plate, and small fluid-filled tubes running through the box.

flexible fuel vehicle
A vehicle that can operate on any mixture of alternative *fuels and *petroleum fuels.

flocculation
The process by which clumps of solids in water or *sewage form through biological or chemical action so they can be separated from water or sewage.

flood
The temporary inundation of land not normally submerged from the overflow of streams or other water bodies.

floodplain
The flat area adjacent to a river or stream that is subject to periodic *flooding.

floor area ratio (FAR)
The gross floor area of a building on a site divided by the total site area.

floorspace
The enclosed area within the walls of a building.

flow rate
The volume of *fluid flowing past a point in a given period of time.

flue gas
The gases coming out of a chimney after *combustion.

fluid
Liquid or gas.

fluidized bed combustion
A process for controlling pollutant emissions from burning coal by using a stream of hot air to suspend powdered coal and sulfur-absorbing limestone particles in a turbulent airflow during *combustion.

fluorinated gas
A group of manmade gases with powerful *global warming potential used as substitutes for *ozone-depleting substances. *See also* hydrofluorocarbon; perfluorocarbon; sulfur hexafluoride.

fluorocarbon
A group of carbon-fluorine compounds including *chlorofluorocarbons and other *ozone-depleting substances.

fluvial geomorphology
The study of the shape of streams and their influence on the land around them. *See also* geomorphology; stream geometry.

flux
In general, a flow.
1 (ecology) The movement of a substance between pools or reservoirs.
2 (energy) The rate of *energy transfer through a surface.
3 (light) The quantity of light *energy per time, measured in *lumens.

fly ash
Noncombustible particles that form in *flue gases. *Compare* bottom ash.

Food and Agriculture Organization (FAO)
The agency of the *United Nations focused on global hunger.

food chain
A linear sequence of feeding relationships. *Compare* food web.

food desert
An urban area in which residents do not have ready access to healthy food.

food forest
A small-scale form of *agroforestry in a multi-story combination of food-bearing trees, shrubs, perennials, and annuals. *See also* homegarden.

food hub
An *organization that manages the aggregation, distribution, and marketing of local and regional food products.

food loss
A decrease in the quantity or quality of food. *See also* food waste.

Food Loss & Waste Protocol
A global accounting and reporting standard for quantifying food loss and waste.

food miles
The distance from where a product is grown to where it is eaten.

food policy
*Public policy concerning the production, distribution, and consumption of food.

food policy council
A formal or informal *organization that writes or oversees local food policy.

food security
The state of having access at all times to sufficient, nutritionally adequate, and safe foods that meet dietary needs and food preferences.

foodshed
A geographic area within which the food for a *population is produced, transported, and consumed.

food sovereignty
The right of people to healthy and culturally appropriate food along with

their right to define their own food and *agriculture *systems.

food system
All the processes involved in the production, processing, transport, and consumption of food, together with the governance, economics, and environmental costs and benefits of food production.

food waste
The discarding or other nonfood use of food that is safe and nutritious for human consumption. *See also* food loss.

food web
A network of feeding relationships in an *ecosystem. *Compare* food chain.

footcandle
A measure of *illuminance equivalent to one *lumen per square foot. *See also* lux.

footlambert
A unit of measure for *luminance or intensity of light being emitted or reflected from a surface.

footprint
The land or water area covered by a project. *Compare* ecological footprint; carbon footprint; water footprint.

foraging
The practice of gathering food found in public or common spaces.

force
A push or pull of one body acting on another body.

forcing mechanism
A process that alters the *energy balance of the *climate system, such as volcanic eruptions and an *enhanced greenhouse effect.

Fordism
The mass production of affordable *consumer goods based on the mass production system developed by Henry Ford.

forecasting
The use of data from the past to make predictions about future trends. *Compare* backcasting.

forest
A *vegetation type dominated by trees.

forest plantation
A forested area established by planting or seeding, typically of one even-aged species.

forestry
The professional management of *forests.

Forest Stewardship Council (FSC)
A nonprofit *organization which promotes environmentally appropriate, socially beneficial, and economically viable management of *forests through *certification of wood products. *See also* chain of custody.

formaldehyde
A colorless, *volatile organic compound and probable *carcinogen used in building materials and furnishings.

form-based code
An alternative to land-use zoning that regulates the form and scale of buildings, streets, and public spaces rather than land use.

fossil fuel
Combustible geologic deposits formed from partially decomposed remains of organisms trapped in the Earth's crust and converted to *coal, *oil, and *natural gas by exposure to heat and pressure.

four laws of ecology
Informal set of principles written by Barry Commoner in 1971: Everything is connected to everything else; everything must go somewhere; nature knows best; and there is no such thing as a free lunch.

four nines
Informal term for a level of *pollutant removal where purity is 99.99%.

fracking *See* hydraulic fracturing.

fractal
An infinitely complex pattern that is self-similar across scales.

fractionation
The distillation process in which *crude oil is refined; each resulting type of *hydrocarbon is called a fraction.

fragmentation
The breaking up of a habitat *patch into two or more smaller pieces, usually by human activities such as *agriculture, urban development, or roads.

frame
A metaphor that structures one's understanding of the world.

Framework Convention on Climate Change *See* UN Framework Convention on Climate Change.

freedom
The range of options available to a person in deciding the kind of life to lead.

free rider
One who benefits from a *public good without paying a share of the cost of its provision and maintenance.

freight modes
Methods of shipping goods which include truck, air, marine, rail, and pipeline freight modes but not gas and water pipelines. *Compare* passenger modes.

French intensive agriculture *See* biointensive agriculture.

Freon
Trade name for a series of *chlorofluorocarbons.

frequency
The number of waves per unit of time. *See also* Hertz.

fresh water
Water other than seawater; water that is not salty.

frost-heaving
The process in which soil freezes and expands, then thaws and contracts.

FSC *See* Forest Stewardship Council.

fuel
A substance that stores *energy.

fuel cell
A device that generates an electrical *current by converting the *chemical energy of a *fuel supplied from outside the cell into *electrical energy.

fuel-cell vehicle (FCV)
A vehicle powered by a *hydrogen *fuel cell and electric motors.

fuel rod
A rod made of uranium that supplies the *fuel for *fission in a nuclear reactor.

fuel switching
Substituting one *fuel for another to do the same task.

fuelwood
Any unprocessed woody biomass used to *fuel a small fire, often for cooking or warmth. *See also* industrial fuelwood.

fugitive dust
The dust released from *nonpoint sources.

fugitive emissions
The release of gases which bypass emission-control equipment.

Fukushima
The site of a *nuclear power plant in Japan where nuclear reactors melted down following an earthquake and tsunami in 2011.

full cost
The cost of a good or service which includes both internal and external costs. *See also* externality.

functional recycling *See* recycling, functional.

fungi
Multicellular nonphotosynthetic organisms which get their energy and nutrients by absorbing materials from their environment; one of the five *kingdom classifications.

fungicide
A type of *pesticide formulated to kill *fungi.

furans
A family of *toxic compounds similar to *dioxins, formed as by-products of *combustion and industrial processes.

fusion
The joining of light nuclei to make a heavier *element and produce *energy; the process which powers stars. *Compare* fission.

G

Gaia theory

The theory that the Earth is an evolving, self-regulating system that maintains conditions favorable to life; led to the field of *Earth system science.

galaxy

One of billions of structures in the universe each consisting of billions of stars, together with gas and dust, held together by gravitational attraction. *See also* galaxy cluster; galaxy supercluster.

galaxy cluster

A structure consisting of hundreds to thousands of *galaxies, held together by gravitational attraction. *See also* galaxy supercluster.

galaxy supercluster

A structure consisting of chains of *galaxy clusters.

Gantt chart

A graphical project schedule which shows each step on a separate line so time overlaps can be seen.

gap analysis

The comparison of *conservation goals, biophysical data, and existing protected areas to identify gaps in *ecosystem protection.

garbage

Animal and vegetable waste resulting from food handling, storage, preparation, and serving.

Garbage Patch *See* Great Pacific Garbage Patch.

gasification

The conversion of *biomass or *fossil fuel into a gas for use as a *fuel, done at high temperatures with a controlled amount of oxygen. *See also* coal gasification.

gasifier

A device in which *gasification is done.

gasohol

Vehicle *fuel consisting of a mix of *gasoline and *ethanol.

gasoline

A complex mixture of relatively volatile hydrocarbons derived from *fractionation, blended to form a *fuel for internal *combustion engines. Also known as motor *gasoline.

gate to gate

The scope of a partial *life cycle assessment that looks at only a single process or material in the product chain.

Gaylord box
A heavy corrugated-cardboard pallet-size box sometimes used for collecting *waste and *recycling materials.

GCM *See* general circulation model; global climate model.

GDH *See* Gross Domestic Happiness.

GDP *See* gross domestic product.

gene
The unit of heredity passed from parent to offspring; a segment of DNA that contains information for *synthesizing a specific protein.

general circulation model (GCM)
A three-dimensional computer *model of the *climate system used in global climate prediction and assessment; a type of *global climate model.

generalist
A species that can feed on many different species and survive in many different habitats. *Compare* specialist.

generally recognized as safe (GRAS)
In the US, a category of food additives that are exempt from Federal Food, Drug, and Cosmetic Act requirements because of either published scientific evidence or a history of use before 1958.

generation
(energy) The process of producing *electric energy by transforming other forms of *energy.

generator
A device that converts *mechanical energy into *electrical energy.

genset
Short for generator set; a combination of a diesel engine and a *generator used to produce *electricity.

genetically modified organism (GMO)
An organism whose genetic code has been altered using a technique called recombinant DNA technology. *See also* genetic engineering.

genetic diversity
The range and relative abundance of *genes among organisms within a given *species.

genetic drift
The gradual loss of genetic variation in a small *population due to random events.

genetic engineering
The manipulation of an organism's genetic material by adding, deleting, or changing segments of its DNA. *See also* genetically modified organism.

gengas *See* synthetic gas.

genius loci
The spirit of a place; its distinctive character.

Genuine Progress Indicator (GPI)
A measure of economic progress that considers improvement in *well-being and quality of life, proposed as an alternative to *Gross Domestic Product. *See also* Index of Sustainable Economic Welfare.

geoengineering
The use of technology to change the dynamics of the *Earth system in order to mitigate *climate destabilization.

geoexchange system
Short for geothermal exchange; the exchange of *heat energy between the earth and an indoor environment. *See also* earth tube; ground-source heat pump.

geographic information systems (GIS)
Computer software which combines maps and databases, with information stored on layers.

geologic time scale
The system of dividing Earth's 4.55-billion-year history into eons, eras, periods, and *epochs based on evidence of past events found in geologic strata. *See also* International Commission on Stratigraphy; stratigraphy.

geomembrane
A *landfill liner made of fabric or porous plastic that allows gases and water to escape but holds in solids.

geomorphology
The study of forms of the Earth's surface and the processes that developed those forms.

geonet
A porous liner made of *synthetic material that facilitates drainage.

georeference
To establish the relationship between coordinates on a map or aerial photograph and a ground system of geographic coordinates.

geosphere
The entire solid matter of the Earth, including the *core, the *mantle, and the *crust.

geotextile
Any synthetic fabric used to prevent *erosion, promote drainage, or serve as a membrane between soil and *aggregate layers.

geothermal
Related to *heat from the Earth's interior.

geothermal energy
Heat from inside the Earth. *See also* geothermal heating and cooling; geothermal power.

geothermal gradient
The rate at which the interior Earth's *temperature increases with depth.

geothermal heating and cooling
The movement of *heat energy to and from the Earth's *thermal mass to *heat or cool and indoor environment. *See also* earth tube; ground-source heat pump.

geothermal plant
A *power plant which uses *heat from Earth's interior to drive a steam turbine.

geothermal power
The production of *electricity using *heat energy from Earth's interior.

gigaton (Gt)
One billion tons.

Gini coefficient
A measure of the degree of income inequality, measured on a scale of 0 to 1.

GIS *See* geographic information systems.

glacial drift *See* glacial till.

glacial period
A period of time when large areas of the Earth were covered by *ice sheets and *glaciers. Also known as *glaciation. *See also* ice age. *Compare* interglacial period.

glacial till
Unsorted earth and rocks deposited directly from glacial ice.

glaciation
An expansion of *ice sheets and *glaciers. *See also* ice age; glacial period.

glacier
A mass of ice derived from compressed snow that shows evidence of movement from higher to lower ground.

glare
Excessive brightness or contrast of brightnesses that interferes with vision.

glazing
A transparent or translucent covering, usually glass, placed in an opening in a building; also known as a window.

gleaning
The practice of gathering food from leftover crops in farmers' fields.

global
The geographic realm encompassing all of Earth.

global climate
The average *climate around the world.

global climate model (GCM)
General term for a three-dimensional computer *model of the *climate system used in *global climate prediction and assessment. See also general circulation model.

global hectare
A hectare of global average biological *productivity. See also Ecological Footprint.

globalization
The increasing integration of economies and societies around the world, particularly through trade and financial flows, and the transfer of culture and technology.

global positioning system (GPS)
A global satellite-based utility which provides users with positioning, navigation, and timing services.

Global Reporting Initiative (GRI)
A widely used, consensus-based international standard for sustainability reporting, with detailed guidelines for measuring and reporting on environmental, *economic, and social dimensions of an *organization's activities.

global warming
An average increase in the *temperature of the *atmosphere near the Earth's surface.

global warming potential (GWP)
A ratio that indicates the *greenhouse effect of a particular gas relative to that of the same quantity of *carbon dioxide over a fixed period of time, usually 100 years.

GMO See genetically modified organism.

GNH See Gross National Happiness.

goal
A statement of measurable desired outcomes. See also mission statement; objective; strategy; vision.

governance
The process of decision-making by which an *organization or society regulates activities and exercises control over resources; often refers to collective actions of multiple stakeholders working together in order to achieve common goals.

GPI See Genuine Progress Indicator.

GPS See global positioning system.

graded
Aggregate which is sorted by size.

gradient
The rate of slope of the land, expressed as a percentage.

grading
The mechanical process of moving earth to modify the surface. *See also* cut; fill.

grant
An award of money for the public good such as research and projects with environmental, *economic, or social benefits.

GRAS *See* generally recognized as safe.

grasshopper effect
The global movement of *pollutants through cycles of *evaporation, *condensation, and transport by global air currents. Also known as the distillation effect.

grassland
A terrestrial *biome in regions with 10 to 30 inches of annual average *precipitation, enough to support grass and small plants but not enough to support large stands of trees.

grassroots
A *metaphor to describe a movement or project that begins with people at the most basic level of an *organization, rather than with its leaders.

gravel
Coarse particles of rock, typically larger than 2 mm in diameter.

gray air
Informal term for gray-colored *photochemical smog which forms in industrial areas without strong sunlight.

grayfield
A previously developed property that is not contaminated to the extent of a *brownfield.

gray infrastructure
Informal term for gutters and pipes used to convey *stormwater.

gray water
The volume of *fresh water required to assimilate *pollution. *Compare* graywater.

graywater
Untreated *wastewater collected from bathroom sinks, showers, bathtubs, and clothes washers which has not come into contact with toilet waste. *Compare* blackwater; gray water.

grazer
An animal in an aquatic *food web who feeds on aquatic plants, especially *algae growing on surfaces. Also known as a scraper. *Compare* collector; shredder.

Great Acceleration
The dramatic acceleration of human impacts including *population, resource use, and environmental deterioration beginning in the years following World War II.

Great Oxidation Event
A *mass extinction that occurred about 2 billion years ago when photosynthetic *cyanobacteria began emitting *oxygen, wiping out most *anaerobic bacteria living on the planet then.

Great Pacific Garbage Patch
A collection of mostly *plastic marine debris trapped in the North Pacific *gyre.

Great Transition
Term sometimes given to a potential next stage of human civilization, away from an industrial age built upon *fossil fuel and *economic growth and toward a *steady-state economy within a regenerative, *sustainable society. Also known as the fifth great turning.

green

General term for an environmentally responsible approach; a metaphor based on the color of most plants.

greenbelt

A zone of trees and other *vegetation that serves as a *buffer between developed and undeveloped land.

green building

An energy- and water-efficient building made of nontoxic and often locally sourced materials that is environmentally responsible and healthy for its occupants; also known as a high-performance building.

green burial *See* eco-cemetery.

green chemistry

The use of chemical materials and processes with little or no *toxicity.

green-collar job

Informal term for a job in an industry related to *sustainable practices, such as *renewable energy.

green economy

An *economy that results in improved human well-being and social equity while operating within Earth's *carrying capacity.

green façade

A type of *green wall in which plants are rooted in the ground and grow upward on trellises or cables. *Compare* living wall.

greenfield

*Open space that has never been built upon.

Green Globes

A green building rating system similar to *LEED, used primarily in Canada.

greenhouse effect

The warming of a planet's surface as a result of certain *atmospheric gases which absorb some of the *infrared solar radiation that would otherwise escape into space and re-radiate this *energy back to the surface.

greenhouse gas

A gas that absorbs *infrared radiation in the *atmosphere; greenhouse gases include *water vapor, *carbon dioxide, *methane, *nitrous oxide, *ozone, and others.

Greenhouse Gas Protocol

The internationally recognized, standardized method for measuring and reporting *climate impact.

green infrastructure

*Open spaces and planted areas used in *stormwater management.

green manure

Freshly cut or still growing green *vegetation that is turned under while still green to return humus and nitrogen to soil. *Compare* manure. *See also* cover crop.

green power

*Electricity generated from *renewable sources.

green purchasing *See* environmentally preferable purchasing.

Green Revolution

The intensification of global food production in the mid-twentieth century based on technologies such as *fertilizers, *pesticides, *irrigation, and high-yield crop varieties.

green revolving loan fund

An internal fund that uses cost savings from sustainability projects to finance other projects.

green roof
A kind of roof covering made of a waterproof layer, growing medium, and plants.

green tag *See* renewable energy certificate.

green tax
A tax levied on environmentally harmful activities and products. *See also* carbon tax; tax shifting. *Compare* feebate; subsidy.

green technology
A *technology that offers a more environmentally benign approach compared to an existing technology.

green wall
A wall covered with plants. *See also* green façade; living wall.

greenwashing
The use of deliberately misleading terms in order to portray an environmentally responsible image.

green water
Rainwater that *infiltrates the soil and is available to plants.

greenway
A large-scale linear *landscape or *corridor.

greywater *See* graywater.

GRI *See* Global Reporting Initiative.

grid
A network of interconnected transmission and distribution lines that distributes *electricity from *power generation stations to users.

Gross Domestic Happiness (GDH)
An index which measures social *well-being and aggregated national

happiness as an alternative to *gross domestic product. *See also* Gross National Happiness.

gross domestic product (GDP)
A measure of *economic growth consisting of the total value of goods and services produced within the boundaries of a country.

Gross National Happiness (GNH)
An index developed by the king of Bhutan which measures that nation's social *well-being and aggregated national happiness as an alternative to *gross domestic product. *See also* Gross Domestic Happiness.

ground-level ozone *See* ozone, ground-level.

ground penetrating radar
A geophysical method that uses high-frequency *electromagnetic waves to develop images of the subsurface.

ground-source heat pump
A *heat pump that transfers heat to and from the Earth's *thermal mass to heat or cool and indoor environment. *See also* earth tube; geothermal heating and cooling.

ground truth
To physically confirm on the ground information provided by calculation or *remote sensing.

groundwater
Water that has accumulated in saturated *soil or rock below the Earth's surface.

groundwater banking
Part of a system for improving water supply reliability by *recharging a *groundwater basin during wet periods

to store water in an *aquifer for later use during dry periods. *See also* conjunctive use.

groundwater flow
*Subsurface movement of water in the saturated zone from areas of *recharge to areas of discharge.

group net metering
A billing arrangement that allows a group of people who generate their own *electricity to sell excess electricity to the local *power *utility. *See also* net metering.

group process
Any of several techniques used to foster group interaction, problem-solving, and achievement of group goals.

grout curtain
A physical barrier for containing *pollutants formed by injecting a *cementlike *chemical into the ground.

growth
An increase in size or an increase in production; growth is a quantitative measure. *See also* economic growth.

growth ring *See* tree ring.

Gt *See* gigaton.

guard rail, planetary
A concept to describe damage limits whose transgression would have intolerable or even catastrophic consequences, such as a 2°C limit for global climate warming.

guerilla gardening
The act of growing flowers or food on private or public land without the consent of the owner.

guild
A group of organisms that perform similar roles within an ecological *community.

gully
A narrow, steep-sided trench formed by *erosion.

gutter
A paved channel. *Compare* swale.

GWP *See* global warming potential.

gyre
A large, circular circulation pattern at the surface of an ocean.

H

Haber-Bosch process
A chemical method of fixing nitrogen used for producing synthetic *fertilizer. *See also* nitrogen fixation.

habitat
The physical environment where an organism lives and finds food, water, cover, and space to grow and reproduce.

habitat conservation plan
A cooperative agreement between *conservation and business *stakeholders which protects parts of *habitats containing *endangered species while allowing landowners to develop in designated adjacent areas.

habitat corridor *See* corridor.

habitat fragmentation *See* fragmentation.

habitat patch *See* patch.

Hadley cell
A large-scale circulation of air through the entire depth of the *troposphere in the lower latitudes, with air flowing toward the equator near the surface and poleward at higher altitudes. *Compare* Ferrel cell; polar cell.

half-life
1 The time required for half of all the nuclei of a *radioactive *element to decay.
2 The time required for a *pollutant to lose half of its original *concentration.

halocarbons
Compounds with powerful *global warming potential containing carbon and either chlorine, fluorine, bromine, or iodine; used in flame retardants.

halons
Compounds containing carbon, bromine, and fluorine; used in fire extinguishers. Also known as bromofluorocarbons. *See also* ozone-depleting substance.

happiness economics
The field of study which analyzes levels of satisfaction and human *well-being relative to *economic well-being.

Happy Planet Index
An index which integrates national measures of social *well-being and *Ecological Footprint. *See also* Gross Domestic Happiness; Gross National Happiness.

HAPs *See* hazardous air pollutants.

hazard
A phenomenon or activity that can cause damage, disease, injury, or death. *Compare* risk.

hazardous air pollutants (HAPs)
A list of *chemicals identified by the *EPA which are considered particularly dangerous.

hazardous material
A substance which poses a risk to humans or the environment when transported. May be known as hazmat. *Compare* hazardous waste.

hazardous waste
A discarded *hazardous material which is *toxic, poisonous, explosive, corrosive, flammable, or infectious.

haze
Particles or vapor suspended in air that impair visibility in all directions over a large area.

hazmat
Short for *hazardous materials.

HCFCs *See* hydrochlorofluorocarbons.

HDD *See* heating degree day.

HDI *See* Human Development Index.

HDPE *See* high-density polyethylene.

head
1   The vertical height that water drops.
2   The depth of water which exerts water pressure on a turbine.

health
A state of complete physical, mental, and social *well-being; not merely the absence of disease or infirmity.

heat
Kinetic energy of atoms and molecules that flows as a result of a *temperature difference. *See also* heat transfer; latent heat; sensible heat.

heat capacity
The amount of *heat required to raise the *temperature of a substance by 1 degree.

heat content
The amount of *heat released per unit of mass upon complete *combustion.

heat exchanger
Any device that transfers *heat from one *fluid to another.

heating degree day (HDD)
The number of degrees per day that the average 24-hour daily temperature is below 65°F, used to estimate heating requirements.

heating load
Heat loss; the rate at which *heat must be added to a space to maintain constant *temperature and *humidity. *Compare* cooling load.

heating penalty
An increased need for heating in winter in some buildings which have *cool roofs.

heating, ventilation, and air conditioning *See* HVAC.

heat island *See* urban heat island effect.

heat island effect *See* urban heat island effect.

heat loss
The rate at which *heat flows out of a space. *See also* heat load.

heat pump
A refrigeration machine with a reversing valve, used to transfer *heat into a building to provide heating or out of a building to provide cooling.

heat recovery system

A process that captures and reuses waste heat in an *HVAC system with some form of *heat exchanger.

heat transfer fluid

A gas or liquid that transmits *heat, such as in a *solar collector or *geothermal power system.

heat wave

A period of abnormally hot weather.

heavy metal

A metal which has a high atomic weight, such as *lead, *mercury, and *arsenic.

heavy oil

An *unconventional oil with high *viscosity and high density.

hectare

A land area of 10,000 square meters, the equivalent of a square 100 meters on a side; equal to 2.47 acres.

hedgerow

A managed strip of plants, shrubs, and trees, usually along a boundary such as a fence line.

heliostat

A device with a movable mirror that reflects solar rays.

hemp

The fiber of non-psychoactive varieties of the cannabis plant used to make paper, canvas, and other textiles, rope, and *biofuel. Also known as industrial hemp.

hempcrete

A lightweight cementitious insulating material made from *hemp hurds, lime binder, and water.

hemp hurds

The woody inner core of the hemp plant stem with short fibers used in making paper and *hempcrete.

HEPA filter

High-efficiency particulate air, also known as high-efficiency particulate arrestance, a type of air filter which removes fine *particulate matter down to 0.3 μm (0.3 micrometers) in size. Referred to by its acronym, HEPA.

herbicide

A type of chemical *pesticide designed to kill or interrupt the normal growth processes of plants.

Hertz

A measure of *frequency equal to one wave or cycle per second.

heterogeneity

The state of a system or process which is composed of dissimilar or diverse elements or properties. *Compare* homogeneity.

heterotroph

An organism that consumes plants or other photosynthesizers. Also known as a *consumer.

HFCs *See* hydrofluorocarbons.

hierarchy

A system consisting of multiple subsystems or levels.

high-density polyethylene (HDPE)

A *polymer used in the manufacture of food and other containers. Its *resin identification code is 2.

high-efficiency particulate air filter *See* HEPA filter.

high-performance building

An energy- and water-efficient building made of nontoxic and often locally sourced materials that is environmentally responsible and healthy for its occupants; also known as a *green building.

high seas

The oceans outside each nation's exclusive economic zone or territorial waters; outside national jurisdictions.

HIPPO

Acronym referring to the primary *drivers of *extinction: *habitat destruction, *invasive species, *pollution, *population, and *overexploitation.

historical baseline *See* baseline.

holding pond

A pond or reservoir, usually made of earth, built to store polluted *runoff. *See also* detention basin.

holistic

Concerned with wholes or integrated *systems rather than with their parts.

Holocene

The geological *epoch extending from around 12,000 years ago to the present.

homegarden

A *food forest in a tropical region.

homeostasis

A characteristic of a system that regulates its internal *environment regardless of changes in the external environment.

homogeneity

The state of a *system or process which is composed of identical elements or properties. *Compare* heterogeneity.

horizon *See* soil horizon.

horizontal well

An *unconventional oil *extraction method in which a well is started vertically and then turned to horizontal at a depth to follow a particular rock stratum or *reservoir.

horsepower (hp)

A unit of *power equal to 550 foot-pounds per second, the amount of *energy required to lift 550 pounds one foot in one second; equivalent to 746 *watts.

hotspot *See* biodiversity hotspot.

household

A family, individual, or group of up to nine unrelated persons, occupying the same housing unit.

housing unit *See* dwelling unit.

hp *See* horsepower.

hub

The central portion of the rotor to which the blades of a *wind turbine are attached. *See also* food hub.

Hubbert curve

The pattern showing the cumulative extraction of a *nonrenewable resource over time. *See also* peak oil; reserve; resource.

Human Development Index (HDI)

An index that assesses a country's progress regarding social and economic development as a composite of life expectancy, education, and *gross domestic product per capita.

human ecology

The study of human *communities and their interactions with their *environment.

humidity

A measure of the density of water vapor per volume of air.

humus

Partially or wholly decayed plant or animal matter. *Compare* compost.

hunting and gathering
A method of livelihood in which most or all food is obtained from undomesticated plants and animals.

hurricane
A *cyclone which forms in the Atlantic or Pacific oceans off North America. *Compare* typhoon.

HVAC
Acronym for heating, ventilation, and air-conditioning, the system or systems that *condition air in a building.

hybrid vehicle
A vehicle that employs two sources of propulsion, usually one that combines an internal *combustion engine with an electric motor and batteries. *Compare* electric vehicle.

hybrid vehicle, plug-in electric *See* plug-in hybrid electric vehicle.

hydrate
A *clathrate in which the cage-forming molecule is water. *See also* methane hydrate.

hydraulic conductivity
The rate at which water can move through a *permeable medium.

hydraulic fracturing
The fracturing of *fossil-fuel-bearing rock using fluids injected underground at high pressures. Also known as fracking.

hydraulic gradient
The direction of *groundwater flow due to changes in the depth of the *water table.

hydric soil
*Soil that is saturated long enough during the growing season to develop *anaerobic conditions in the upper layer.

hydrocarbon
A substance containing only *hydrogen and carbon, such as *fossil fuels.

hydrochlorofluorocarbons (HCFCs)
Compounds containing *hydrogen, fluorine, chlorine, and carbon *atoms, introduced as temporary, less damaging replacements for *chlorofluorocarbons; HCFCs are also *ozone-depleting substances and *greenhouse gases.

hydrodynamics
The study of the dynamics of fluids in motion, such as tides or water moving through a *watershed.

hydroelectric dam *See* dam; hydroelectric power.

hydroelectric plant
A *power plant in which the *energy of falling or flowing water spins a *turbine *generator to produce *electricity.

hydroelectric power
*Electrical energy produced by falling or flowing water. *See* hydroelectric plant; *see also* microhydropower.

hydrofluorocarbons (HFCs)
Compounds containing only *hydrogen, fluorine, and carbon *atoms, introduced as alternatives to *ozone-depleting substances; powerful *greenhouse gases with high *global warming potentials.

hydrogen
An element with one *proton and one *electron. Abundant in stars and all living things; used as an *energy carrier for *fuel cells.

hydrograph
A streamflow graph that shows the change in discharge over time.

hydrologic cycle
The continuous movement of water through the *reservoirs of water in the *Earth system by *evaporation, *condensation, *precipitation, and the flow of rivers and *groundwater.

hydrology
The study of the properties, distribution, and circulation of water.

hydrolysis
The decomposition of a *compound by interaction with water.

hydronic
A heating or cooling system using heated or cooled water.

hydropower *See* hydroelectric power.

hydrosphere
All of the liquid water in the *Earth system.

hyperaccumulator
A plant which can accumulate larger amounts of micronutrients than most other plants.

hyphae
Microscopic filaments of *fungi which absorb nutrients. *See also* mycelium.

hyporheic zone
The subsurface environment below a stream channel.

hypothesis
The first step in the *scientific method, a proposed explanation of a phenomenon that can be tested scientifically.

hypoxia
The condition of low dissolved oxygen *concentrations in water.

I

IAQ *See* indoor air quality.

ice age
A long-term reduction in the temperature of the Earth's climate, resulting in an expansion of *ice sheets and *glaciers. *See also* glacial period.

iceberg
A piece of ice that has broken off the end of a *glacier and is floating in open water. *See also* calving.

ice core
A cylinder of ice obtained by drilling into a *glacier or *ice sheet, used to study past *climate conditions.

ice house
A small building used to store ice for preserving food or for cooling during hot weather before the invention of modern refrigeration.

ice sheet
A mass of land ice of continental size derived from compressed snow. *Compare* glacier.

ice shelf
A slab of ice of considerable thickness at the margin of a continent, attached to land and floating on the sea.

ICLEI
An *organization of cities, towns, counties, metropolitan governments, and local government associations known as Local Governments for Sustainability; originally known as the International Council of Local Environment Initiatives.

IEA *See* International Energy Agency.

illegal, unreported, and unregulated fishing (IUU)
Fishing conducted in violation of national laws or internationally agreed conservation and management measures.

illuminance
Light striking a surface; measured in *footcandles.

immiscible liquid
A liquid that does not mix with water. *Compare* miscible.

impact
The effect or influence of an action.

imperialism
The policy or practice of extending power over land and other people through military or political force.

impervious surface
A surface such as paving or rooftop that prevents water from *infiltrating soil. *Compare* permeable surface.

impoundment
A body of water confined by a *dam or other barrier.

inbreeding depression
A condition in which close relatives mate with each other and produce weak or defective offspring as a result.

incandescent light bulb
A *lamp in which electric *current heats a filament, thereby producing light.

incentive
An economic or material reward in return for acting in a particular way which is beneficial to a set goal. *Compare* disincentive.

incinerator
A large furnace used for burning *waste.

incrementalism
An approach which implements change in multiple small steps gradually over time rather than attempting radical innovations.

independent power producer
An entity which is not a *utility that owns or operates facilities for generating *electricity for use primarily by the public.

index
A composite indicator which combines multiple sources of data into one number.

Index of Sustainable Economic Welfare (ISEW)
An economic indicator designed to measure the overall impact of economic

activity on human *well-being as an alternative to *Gross Domestic Product. *See also* Genuine Progress Indicator.

indicator
A representative factor which indicates the condition or functioning of a characteristic or a *system, used to measure progress toward a goal.

indicator species
A *species whose presence indicates particular environmental conditions.

indigenous
Existing, growing, or produced naturally in a region; *native to a region.

indigenous peoples
*Communities or nations who are descendants of peoples who inhabited a territory prior to colonization or establishment of the present state, or whose cultural patterns and social institutions differ from the dominant societies in which they live, and who consider themselves distinct from the prevailing sectors of society.

indirect gain
A strategy for *passive solar heating in which a *thermal mass is located between the interior space and incoming *solar radiation. *See also* roof pond; Trombe wall.

indoor air
The breathable air inside a habitable structure or conveyance.

indoor air quality (IAQ)
The condition of *indoor air relative to human health and comfort.

inductance
The property by which moving an electrical *conductor inside a magnetic field induces *electric current to flow, as in a *generator, and by which

sending current through the conductor inside a magnetic field causes motion, as in an electric motor. *See also* induction.

induction

The process of generating *electrical current in a conductor by moving it inside a magnetic field. *See also* generator; inductance.

inductive reasoning

Logical reasoning from specific observations to a general conclusion. *Compare* deductive reasoning.

industrial ecology

An approach to the design of products and processes that helps an industrial system behave like an *ecosystem, where the output from one industry is the input for another.

industrial food *See* industrialized agriculture.

industrial fuelwood

Any *wood fuel used for industrial purposes.

industrialized agriculture

Large-scale farming using *fossil fuel–driven machinery, large amounts of *irrigation water, *synthetic *fertilizers, *pesticides, and *monoculture planting; also known as agribusiness.

industrial metabolism

The physical processes by which an industry uses *energy, converts raw materials, and produces *waste.

Industrial Revolution

The rapid transition from a rural, agrarian *economy with goods made by craftsmen to an urban, industrial economy, beginning with development of the steam engine powered by *coal in 18th-century Britain and spreading to the rest of the world.

industrial sector

The part of the *economy consisting of manufacturing, mining, construction, *agriculture, *fisheries, and *forestry.

industrial sludge *See* sludge, industrial.

industrial smog *See* smog, industrial.

industrial symbiosis

A network of exchanges in which the output from one industry is the input for another.

industrial waste

The leftover and discarded material produced as a by-product of manufacturing, *extraction, *power generation, and other large-scale commercial enterprises.

infill

The process of building and developing on vacant or under-used parcels in a city where *infrastructure is already in place.

infiltration

The process in which rainwater flows through or is absorbed by pores in *soil.

informal economy

An *economic sector where production and employment take place in unincorporated small or unregistered enterprises without legal or social protection.

information literacy

A set of abilities with which a person can recognize when information is needed and have the ability to locate, evaluate, and effectively use the needed information.

infrared radiation

*Electromagnetic radiation with wavelengths longer than visible *light, felt as *heat.

infrastructure
The technological support *systems used to transport people, goods, water, *waste, *energy, and information in human communities.

infrastructure, ecological See ecological infrastructure.

injection well
A well into which fluids are injected for underground *waste disposal.

inorganic compound
A combination of two or more *elements other than those used to form *organic compounds.

inorganic fertilizer See fertilizer, synthetic.

inorganic pollutant
A category of *contaminants not organic in origin, including inorganic salts and *heavy metals.

insecticide
A type of chemical *pesticide designed to kill or interrupt the normal growth processes of insects.

in situ
In its original position, from the Latin phrase meaning "in position."

insolation
The intensity of incoming *solar radiation; the amount of radiant *energy striking a given surface area in a given time.

institutions
The norms, rules, practices, and conventions that structure human interactions.

instrumental record
The set of direct measurements of Earth's *climate elements including *temperature, pressure, humidity, and *precipitation, as opposed to *climate *proxy records.

instrumental value
The assumption that a thing is valuable only insofar as it benefits humans. Compare intrinsic value.

insulation
A material that resists *heat transfer. See also R-value.

insulator
A material that does not allow electrical *current to flow.

integrated design
A collaborative process of building design by an *interdisciplinary team which provides simultaneous solutions to multiple problems.

integrated pest management (IPM)
An ecologically based strategy which controls insects with minimal use of *pesticides.

integrated waste management
The practice of using multiple approaches including *waste prevention, *recycling, *composting, and *landfill disposal to manage *municipal solid waste.

integrated water resources management (IWRM)
A process which promotes the coordinated development and management of water, land, and related resources to maximize economic and social welfare equitably without compromising ecological *sustainability.

integrated weed management
The control of *weeds through long-term management using multiple strategies including physical, chemical, biological, and cultural control.

integrity, ecological

The state of an *ecosystem which is able to maintain its components, *structure, and function when disturbed.

intensity *See* rainfall intensity.

intensive green roof

A *green roof which is planted in growing medium deeper than 6 inches.

intentional community

A group of people who live together on the basis of explicit common values. *See also* cohousing; ecovillage.

intercropping

The growing of two or more different crops simultaneously in the same area. *See also* polyculture.

interdisciplinary

Involving the use and synthesis of knowledge and methods from two or more traditional fields of study. *Compare* multidisciplinary; silo.

intergenerational equity

The concept that all human generations, including those alive today and those in future, have an equal right to *natural capital, a stable *climate, and a healthy *biosphere. *See also* sustainable development.

interglacial

A period of relatively warmer *climate occurring between *ice ages. *Compare* glacial period.

Intergovernmental Panel on Climate Change (IPCC)

An international group of scientists who assess and synthesize current *peer-reviewed scientific, social, and *economic research relevant to understanding *climate change, its potential *impacts, *mitigation, and *adaptation.

Intergovernmental Platform on Biodiversity and Ecosystem Services (IPBES)

A scientific body for the study of *biodiversity and *ecosystem services similar in structure to the *Intergovernmental Panel on Climate Change.

interior habitat

*Habitat located away from human land uses and large enough not to be influenced by *edge effect.

intermittent stream

A stream that flows only during certain times of the year, for longer periods than an *ephemeral stream. *Compare* perennial stream.

International Commission on Stratigraphy

The scientific body which defines units of the *Geological Time Scale. *See also* Anthropocene epoch; stratigraphy.

International Energy Agency (IEA)

An intergovernmental *organization which acts as an energy policy advisor to *OECD member countries and which publishes data, projections, and analysis. *See also* Energy Information Administration.

International Renewable Energy Agency (IRENA)

An intergovernmental *organization that promotes the use of *renewable energy.

Intertropical Convergence Zone (ITCZ)

A band of low surface pressure where trade winds converge that encircles the globe near the equator; sometimes known informally as the doldrums.

intragenerational equity

The concept that all people in the current generation have an equal right to *natural capital, a stable *climate, and a healthy *biosphere. *Compare* intergenerational equity. *See also* social justice.

intrinsic remediation

The treatment of *soil *pollution by natural processes including *indigenous *bacteria, dilution, and *sorption. Also known as natural *attenuation, natural *bioremediation, or passive bioremediation.

intrinsic value

The assumption that a thing has value in and for itself, regardless of its usefulness to humans. *Compare* instrumental value.

introduction

The release of animals into an area where they did not exist in the past. *See also* captive breeding; reintroduction.

invasive species

A *species introduced outside its normal distribution which increases in abundance at the expense of *native species, interfering with an *ecosystem's normal functioning.

inverter

An electrical device that converts *direct current to *alternating current.

in vitro

Testing or action in an artificial environment outside a living organism or body. *Compare* in vivo.

in vivo

Testing or action within a living organism or body. *Compare* in vitro.

ion

An *atom that has an *electrical charge through the gain or loss of *electrons.

IOU

Acronym for investor-owned *utility.

IPAT formula

An acronym summarizing the drivers of *environmental degradation which says that *impact is a product of *population, affluence, and *technology.

IPBES *See* Intergovernmental Platform on Biodiversity and Ecosystem Services.

IPCC *See* Intergovernmental Panel on Climate Change.

IPM *See* integrated pest management.

IRENA *See* International Renewable Energy Agency.

iron fertilization

A type of *geoengineering in which iron is deliberately introduced to the upper ocean to stimulate *phytoplankton growth with the hope of thereby *sequestering additional *atmospheric *carbon dioxide in the ocean.

irradiance *See* solar irradiance.

irradiation

A food processing method in which food is exposed to a dose of radiation for the purpose of killing *pathogenic bacteria and insects by disrupting their DNA.

irrigation

The controlled application of water to sustain plant growth by means other than natural rainfall.

ISEW *See* Index of Sustainable Economic Welfare.

island biogeography

The study of isolated *habitats; the theory that in isolated habitats as area decreases, the number of *species decreases. *See also* biogeography.

ISO

The short name (but not an acronym) of the International Organization for Standardization, a consensus-based network of national standards institutes which develops international standards.

isoconcentration

A line of equal *contaminant *concentration drawn on a map.

isolated gain

A type of *passive solar heating in which solar collection and storage are thermally isolated from the occupied spaces.

isopleth

The line or area on a map represented by an *isoconcentration.

isotopes

*Atoms of the same *element that have the same the number of *protons but differ in the number of *neutrons.

ITCZ *See* Intertropical Convergence Zone.

IUU *See* illegal, unreported, and unregulated fishing.

IWRM *See* integrated water resources management.

J

jet stream
A relatively narrow band of high-speed wind current in the upper levels of the *troposphere.

Jevons' paradox
The principle that increased *efficiency in the use of a resource tends to increase, rather than decrease, the rate of consumption. Also known as the *rebound effect.

Jo'burg
A nickname for *Earth Summit 2002, the UN World Summit on Sustainable Development held in Johannesburg, South Africa.

Johannesburg Summit *See* Earth Summit 2002.

joule (J)
metric unit of *energy equal to one *watt per second or the *work done by a force of one newton acting through a distance of one meter.

K

Keeling curve

A graph of measurements of *carbon dioxide *concentrations taken at the Mauna Loa Observatory in Hawaii since 1958.

kerogen

A waxy *hydrocarbon found in *oil shale that can be converted to a *heavy oil called *shale oil when heated.

kerosene

A light-colored *fuel oil obtained by *petroleum distillation and used in *lamps, space heaters, and jet engines.

keyline design

A technique for maximizing water resources on farms through landform analysis.

keystone species

A species so critical to an *ecosystem that its removal could cause major disruption for the whole ecosystem.

kilowatt-hour (kWh)

A unit of *energy for measuring the use of *electricity equal to one kilowatt of *power delivered for one hour.

kinetic energy

The *energy of motion.

kingdom

One of five major classifications of organisms in the taxonomic rank below *domain, consisting of *bacteria, *protists, *fungi, plants, and animals.

Kuznets curve, environmental

The hypothesis that various environmental impacts first increase and then eventually decrease as income per capita increases.

Kyoto Protocol

An international treaty adopted in 1997 at the *United Nations Framework Convention on Climate Change and expiring in 2012 which limited *carbon dioxide emissions for those developed countries that signed it.

L

lacustrine
Associated with ponds, lakes, or lake shores.

lagging indicator
An indicator which measures past results.

lagoon
1 A shallow pond constructed for *wastewater treatment.
2 A shallow body of marine water, often separated from the sea by *coral reefs or sandbars.

lake
A large body of standing water.

lamp
An artificial light source.

land cover
The physical coverage of land, usually expressed in terms of *vegetation cover or lack of cover.

land ethic
The philosophy that land itself has *intrinsic value and *moral standing.

landfarming
A type of *bioremediation in which *waste or contaminated soil is spread in a thin layer on the land so that it is easily accessible by *aerobic soil microorganisms.

landfill
A *waste disposal site for long-term storage of *solid waste in which waste is buried. *See also* sanitary landfill.

landfill cell
An area within a *landfill where *waste is deposited, compacted, and covered.

landfill gas (LFG)
*Biogas generated by *anaerobic *decomposition of organic material in a *landfill.

landfill mining
A process of removing and *reclaiming reusable resources from *solid wastes which have previously been landfilled.

landform
Any recognizable physical form of the Earth's surface, having a characteristic shape.

land grab
Large acquisitions of land or water rights in *developing countries by corporations, speculators, and governments that have negative impact on local and marginalized *communities.

landscape
The natural and cultural features that distinguish one part of the surface of the Earth from another part; regional in scale, often considered to be the area one can see from a mountaintop.

landscape ecology
The study of the spatial pattern, structure, and function of *landscapes.

land trust
A nonprofit *organization that works to acquire land, to help others acquire land or *conservation easements, and to provide *stewardship.

land use
Human activities carried out on a given piece of land for a particular purpose.

land use planning
The assignment of *land use categories and the segregation of incompatible activities through *zoning and other development controls.

La Niña
A strong cooling of surface water in the eastern Pacific Ocean that occurs every 2 to 10 years causing a major shift in oceanic and atmospheric circulation. *Compare* El Niño; *see also* El Niño/ Southern Oscillation.

large woody debris
Fallen trees, logs, root wads, and limbs that fall into streams, rivers, and lakes. Also known as coarse woody debris.

latent heat
*Heat energy that changes the state of matter from solid to liquid or from liquid to gas without a change in *temperature; released when gas condenses or liquid freezes. *Compare* sensible heat. *See also* condensation; evaporation.

lava
*Magma which reaches the Earth's surface.

Law of the Sea Convention
An international agreement by which governments maintain order, productivity, and peaceful relations on the sea, including the establishment of jurisdictional limits.

laws of ecology *See* four laws of ecology.

LC50
The lethal *concentration of a substance required to kill 50% of a test population.

LCA *See* life cycle assessment.

LD50
The dose of a toxicant required to kill 50% of a test population.

LDC *See* Least Developed Countries.

LDPE *See* low-density polyethylene.

leachate
Liquid in a *landfill consisting of rainwater, liquid from *organic waste, and dissolved *pollutants.

leaching
The process by which solid materials are dissolved in a liquid and *transported to another location.

lead
A *toxic *heavy metal.

leading indicator
An indicator which predicts future trends; *statistics that change before their results change.

leakage
Material that does not follow an intended pathway, such as loss of water through a crack in a *dam or litter escaping from a *waste stream.

leapfrog technology

A technology designed in a developed country and adopted in a developing country, accelerating *sustainable development by skipping over and not adopting an intermediate unsustainable technology previously used by developed countries.

Least Developed Countries (LDC)

A list of low-income countries designated by the *United Nations which confront the most severe impediments to sustainable development. Criteria are income per capita; health, education, and literacy; and *economic vulnerability.

LED *See* light-emitting diode.

LEED

Leadership in Energy and Environmental Design, a *green building *certification system.

less than a load (LTL)

A truck delivery in which the trailer is not full.

LETS *See* local exchange trading system.

levee

A natural or artificial embankment along a stream that prevents flooding of the land behind it.

LFG *See* landfill gas.

lichen

A plant-like combination of *symbiotic organisms consisting of a *fungus plus an *alga, a *cyanobacterium, or both.

LID *See* low-impact development.

life cycle

The stages of a product or process from raw material acquisition through production, transportation, use, and disposal.

life cycle assessment (LCA)

A method for quantifying the total environmental impacts of a material, product, or building through all phases of its life from *cradle to grave; also known as life cycle analysis.

life cycle cost

All the costs associated with a building or product over its *life cycle, including design, installation, operation, maintenance, and disposal.

lifetime

The approximate amount of time it would take for a *greenhouse gas or other *pollutant to return to its natural level of *concentration.

lift

A layer of *compacted *fill material.

light

The visible portion of the *electromagnetic wave spectrum with wavelengths 400 to 700 nanometers, able to be interpreted by nerve receptors in the human brain.

light-emitting diode (LED)

A semiconductor device used for lighting which consumes less *energy and lasts longer than other current lighting technologies.

light non-aqueous phase liquid (LNAPL)

A *non-aqueous phase liquid with a specific gravity lower than water and which therefore floats above the *water table. Most *petroleum fuels and lubricating oils are LNAPLs.

light pipe

1 (electronics) An optical fiber or transparent rod for transmitting light lengthwise.
2 (buildings) A form of *toplighting; a tube to bring daylight from

a roof into a room. Also known as a solar tube.

light pollution
Any adverse effect of artificial *light, including sky glow, *light trespass, and *glare.

light rail
A metropolitan electric railway system able to operate single cars or short trains along exclusive rights-of-way and to board and discharge passengers at track or car floor level.

light shelf
A light-colored, horizontal projection below a window used to improve the distribution of daylight into an interior space.

light trespass
Unwanted *light that violates property boundaries. *See also* light pollution.

lightweighting
Various strategies for producing vehicles, products, and packaging using less material or lower-weight material in order to improve *fuel efficiency or to reduce embodied *energy and resource *consumption.

light well
A narrow enclosed space in a building for providing natural daylight. *Compare* atrium.

lignin
A class of organic *polymers which bind the woody cell walls in plants.

lignite
A soft grade of *coal used primarily in electric *power plants. Also known as brown coal.

lignocellulose
The inedible parts of plants consisting of *lignin and cellulose, used to make *biofuels.

li-ion battery *See* lithium-ion battery.

limnology
The study of inland waters, including lakes, *rivers, *streams, *wetlands, and *groundwater.

linear Fresnel reflector *See* compact linear Fresnel reflector.

linoleum
A floor covering made from renewable ingredients including *linseed oil, pine rosin, cork dust, wood flour, limestone, mineral pigments, and jute or canvas backing.

linseed oil
An oil extracted from flax seeds.

liquefied natural gas (LNG)
*Natural gas converted to liquid form by cooling to a very low *temperature.

liquefied petroleum gas (LPG)
A mixture of butane, propane, and other light *hydrocarbons produced at refineries or *natural gas processing plants and liquefied by cooling or pressurization to facilitate storage and transportation.

listing
The addition of a *species considered to be facing a high risk of *extinction to a list of *endangered species such as the international IUCN Red List or the lists maintained by the US Fish and Wildlife Service and National Marine Fisheries Service, mandated by the US *Endangered Species Act. *Compare* de-listing.

lithium-ion battery
A type of rechargeable battery in which lithium ions move from the negative electrode to the positive electrode during discharge and from the positive electrode to negative electrode during charge.

lithosphere
The outer layer of Earth composed of the *crust and the rigid upper layer of the *mantle.

litter
1 Undecomposed plant parts such as leaves and twigs on the soil surface.
2 Visible *solid waste discarded outside the normal *waste collection system.

Little Ice Age
An interval of colder temperatures from the 15th to 19th centuries during which mountain *glaciers expanded.

littoral zone
The shallow water at the edge of a lake or *wetland.

Living Building
A stringent *green building *certification system based on the Living Building Challenge.

living fence See hedgerow.

Living Machine
A proprietary biological *wastewater treatment system which uses a series of tanks containing communities of *bacteria, plants, and animals.

Living Planet Index
A measure of the state of the world's biological diversity based on *population trends of vertebrate *species from around the world.

living wage
A wage sufficient to meet the basic living needs of an average-sized family in a particular economy.

living wall
A type of *green wall on which plants are hydroponically grown without soil in vertical modules that receive a steady flow of water and nutrients. *Compare* green façade.

lm See lumen.

LNAPL See light non-aqueous phase liquid.

LNG See liquefied natural gas.

load
The rate at which customers demand *energy from the electric system; the amount of *power delivered to a given point.

load management
Strategies for balancing *electric power demand and supply by shifting *consumption from periods of high demand to periods of lower demand.

loam
*Soil texture which has a relatively even mixture of *sand, *clay, and *silt.

local currency
A medium of exchange designed to be used within one particular community. *See also* complementary currency.

local energy
A locally owned *energy project using locally available *renewable energy sources. *See also* community energy.

local exchange trading system (LETS)
A community-based bartering network in which people can use *local currency or can exchange goods and services without the need for money.

locavore
A person who eats primarily locally produced food.

loess
Windblown *silt and *clay deposits.

LOHAS

Acronym for lifestyles of health and sustainability, a market segment. *See* segmentation.

longwave radiation *See* infrared radiation.

Love Canal

A community in Niagara Falls, New York, where serious health problems from *toxic waste discovered in 1977 led to passage of *Superfund legislation.

low-e *See* low-emissivity coating.

low-emissivity (low-e) coating

A thin film deposited on glazing which admits the full spectrum of sunlight but blocks the escape of *infrared radiation to reduce *heat gain or heat loss.

low-density polyethylene (LDPE)

A soft, flexible *polymer used in the manufacture of containers and plastic film. Its *resin identification code is 4.

low-hanging fruit

An informal term used to describe targets which are easy to achieve and which carry no or low cost.

low-impact development (LID)

*Stormwater management strategies that work with natural *systems to manage stormwater close to its source, including *rain gardens, vegetated *swales, *porous paving, *green roofs, and *constructed wetlands.

LPG *See* liquefied petroleum gas.

LTL *See* less than a load.

lumen (lm)

A measure of the flow of *light *energy emitted by a source.

luminaire

A complete lighting unit including a *lamp, reflectors, and connections. Also known as a *fixture.

luminance

Brightness; the intensity of *light leaving a surface. *See also* footlambert.

luminescent

Emitting *light that is not caused by *heat.

luminosity

The brightness of a *light source of a certain wavelength as it appears to the eye.

lux

A measure of *illuminance equivalent to one *lumen per square meter. *See also* footcandle.

M

macroinvertebrate
An invertebrate visible to the unaided eye including insects, spiders, worms, mollusks, crustaceans, and others.

magma
Molten rock found in the *mantle, below the *crust. *Compare* lava.

magnetic separation
The use of magnets to separate *ferrous materials from *solid waste.

makeup air
Outdoor air brought into a building to replace exhausted air.

makeup water *See* cooling tower makeup water.

management system
The set of procedures which systemizes how things are done in an *organization. *See also* environmental management system.

manhole *See* sewer access.

mantle
The ductile layer of the *geosphere which lies between the *crust and the *core.

manufacturing
The economic sector consisting of *organizations engaged in the mechanical or chemical transformation of materials or substances into new products. Does not include *agriculture, construction, mining, or resource extraction.

manure
Urine and feces of animals that can be used as a form of *organic fertilizer. *Compare* green manure.

marginal benefit
The benefit of one additional unit.

marginal cost
The cost of one additional unit.

marine reserve
An area of the ocean where activities that remove animals or plants or that alter *habitats are prohibited; also known as a no-take marine protected area.

Marine Stewardship Council (MSC)
*Organization that develops *certification standards and provides *eco-labels for wild-capture *fisheries.

market-based instrument
An *economic instrument in which a change in technology or behavior is encouraged through financial incentives such as pricing, taxes, or *subsidies. *See also* carbon tax, emissions trading, tax shifting.

market segmentation *See* segmentation.

marsh
A type of *wetland characterized by herbaceous *emergent vegetation adapted to saturated soil conditions.

mass balance
The application of the principle of the *conservation of matter. *See also* material flow analysis.

mass extinction
An extraordinary *extinction event in which a large proportion of the world's *species become extinct in a relatively short time period.

mass transit *See* public transportation.

material flow analysis (MFA)
A systematic assessment of the inputs and outputs of matter through a *system such as an *ecosystem, a city, an *economy, or an *industrial metabolism.

material intensity per service unit (MIPS)
A calculation which correlates material input and number of service units. *See also* eco-efficiency.

material recovery facility (MRF)
A facility where *recyclable materials are sorted and processed.

material safety data sheet (MSDS)
Detailed information on physical and chemical properties, physical and health hazards, *exposure limits, and handling precautions, required by US law for a *hazardous *chemical.

materials footprint
Informal term for the total material consumption and *waste throughout the *life cycle of a product.

matrix
The dominant *land use type which surrounds *patches and *corridors.

matter
Any physical substance; something which occupies space and has mass.

maximum contaminant level (MCL)
An enforceable *EPA standard for the highest permissible *concentration of a *contaminant in public water supplies.

maximum residue limits (MRL)
The maximum amount of a *pesticide allowed to remain in or on a food.

maximum sustainable yield
The greatest amount of a *renewable natural resource that can be extracted without diminishing the resource over time.

MCL *See* maximum contaminant level.

MDGs *See* Millennium Development Goals.

MEA *See* multilateral environmental agreement.

mean
The sum of numbers in a group divided by the quantity of numbers; also known as average. *See also* median; statistics.

meander
A curve or bend in a river.

meander belt
The zone along which a meandering *stream shifts its channel over time.

mean radiant temperature (MRT)
The average *radiant temperature of all surfaces in a space.

measurement
*Empirical information about a state, quantity, or process.

measurement and verification (M&V)
A written plan which verifies that investments in *energy efficiency measures are providing the benefits expected.

mechanical energy
Energy of motion or position; can be either *kinetic energy or *potential energy.

mechanical system
(buildings) A system which provides *power, water, heating, cooling, ventilation, removal of *sewage, fire protection, or telecommunications in a building.

median
In a range of numbers, the quantity that falls exactly in the middle so that 50% of the cases are above or below. *See also* mean; statistics.

medical waste
Healthcare *waste generated in the research, diagnosis, or treatment of humans or other animals that may be contaminated by potentially infectious materials; does not include *hazardous waste.

megacity
A metropolitan area with a *population of 10 million or more.

megafaunal extinction
The *extinction of the world's largest land mammals during the *Pleistocene epoch, generally attributed to overhunting by humans.

megaton (Mt)
One million tons.

megawatt (MW)
One million *watts.

meltdown
The accidental melting of *fuel rods inside a nuclear *reactor that occurs if coolant stops flowing.

membrane
In a cell, a thin film separating the *cell's contents from the outside and regulating the substances that can enter and leave the cell.

membrane bioreactor
A compact device for *wastewater treatment consisting of a series of tanks where *bacteria living on membranes break down *nutrients.

mercaptan
An organic chemical compound added to *natural gas for safety to give the gas a detectable odor.

mercury
A *toxic *heavy metal.

meta-analysis
A statistical method of combining the results of multiple studies to produce a single conclusion based on a larger sample size.

metabolism
The processes of exchange and *chemical reactions taking place in a *cell, organism, or other *system by which it derives *energy from its surroundings.

metadata
Information about how *data were acquired and their content, quality, and condition; "data about data."

metaphor
A figure of speech in which a descriptive term for one thing is used to suggest a similarity with another thing which it does not literally describe. *Compare* analogy.

metapopulation
A collection of local *populations of the same *species linked by some degree of migration; a "population of populations."

meter *See* electric meter.

methane
A gas produced by *anaerobic *decomposition of organic matter; the major component of *natural gas and a powerful *greenhouse gas.

methane clathrate *See* methane hydrate; *see also* clathrate; hydrate.

methane digester *See* digester.

methane hydrate
A partly frozen mix of *methane gas and ice, usually found in *sediments. *See also* clathrate; hydrate.

methanogens
Various *anaerobic *archaea that produce *methane as a by-product of *metabolism.

methanol
A *toxic alcohol used as an *alternative fuel, gasoline additive, solvent, and *pesticide. Also known as methyl alcohol and wood alcohol.

methanotrophs
*Aerobic *bacteria with the ability to metabolize *methane as their only *carbon and *energy source with *carbon dioxide and water as the by-products.

metric ton
1000 kilograms, equal to 2204.6 pounds.

MFA *See* material flow analysis.

microbiological volatile organic compounds (MVOCs)
Gaseous *organic compounds produced by the *metabolism of mold and *bacteria that can cause olfactory comfort problems in buildings. *See also* volatile organic compounds.

microclimate
A *climate in a small area that is different from the regional climate, formed by effects of topography, moisture, sun, and shade.

microfinance
The providing of financial services to low-income groups or individuals who traditionally lack access to banking and related services.

microgrid
A local, small-scale version of the centralized power *grid featuring many small units rather than one large, central unit. *See also* distributed generation; smart grid.

microhabitat
A very small-scale *habitat.

microhydropower
A *hydroelectric system that generates less than 100 kW of *power.

microorganism
Any organism too small to be seen by the unaided eye, including *archaea, *bacteria, *protists, and many *fungi.

microtopography
Small-scale variations in the shape of the surface of the land, resulting in a diversity of *microhabitats.

microwave
*Electromagnetic radiation with wavelengths longer than *infrared radiation and shorter than short-wave radio wavelengths.

migration
Seasonal movement from one *habitat to another.

Milankovitch cycles
Regularly recurring changes in the tilt of Earth's *axis, *precession of Earth's axis, and *eccentricity of Earth's orbit which influence cycles of *climate cooling and warming.

milestone
An action or event which indicates completion of a scheduled stage in a project timeline.

Millennium Declaration
An agreement of *United Nations members in 2000 which established the *Millennium Development Goals.

Millennium Development Goals
A set of eight goals adopted by *United Nations members in 2000 and aimed at halving extreme *poverty in all its forms, including hunger, illiteracy, and disease, by 2015. *See also* Sustainable Development Goals.

Millennium Ecosystem Assessment
A *United Nations report of *indicators of *ecosystem health, based on a synthesis of global scientific research on *ecosystem services conducted from 2001 to 2005.

mind map
A hierarchical diagram of information that shows a central idea surrounded by connected branches of associated topics. *Compare* concept map.

mine spoils *See* overburden.

mineral
Any naturally occurring inorganic substance found in Earth's *crust as a crystalline solid.

mine tailings *See* tailings.

mining, hardrock
Underground mining of hard minerals, usually containing *metals. Does not include *coal, which is found in softer minerals.

mining, mountaintop removal
A large-scale, environmentally devastating form of strip mining in which rock above a *coal deposit is blasted apart, removed, and deposited in valleys.

mining, open-pit
A type of surface mine in which *ore and *overburden are removed from immense pits.

mining, strip
A type of surface mine in which deep trenches are cut to expose *coal or *minerals found near the surface.

mining, subsurface
A method in which *coal is produced by tunneling underground; also known as underground mining.

mining, surface
The removal of *overburden and extraction of *ore found at or near Earth's surface.

MIPS *See* material intensity per service unit.

miscible
Relating to two or more substances that can be mixed and will remain mixed. *Compare* immiscible liquid.

mission statement
A brief written statement of an *organization's core purpose or reason for existing.

mitigation
1 (*climate change) Measures undertaken to minimize the extent or impact of a problem such as climate change. *See also* climate action plan.
2 (*habitat) A mechanism in which a damaged habitat is rehabilitated or an intact habitat area is set aside to compensate for habitat that is destroyed elsewhere. *See also* mitigation, wetland; mitigation banking.

mitigation banking
The setting aside of *wetland areas in advance of anticipated losses. Banked wetlands provide credits which can be bought and sold, similar to emissions trading. Known as *conservation banking when used with other types of *habitats.

mitochondria
Organelles responsible for generating *energy through *aerobic respiration in all *eukaryotic *cells.

mixed use
An urban pattern in which housing is mixed with other *land uses including schools, shops, businesses, restaurants, and entertainment.

mixing zone
An area of a lake or *river adjacent to a *point source where *pollution levels are allowed to be higher than the acceptable *concentration for the general water body.

mixture
Two or more substances which are combined physically but not chemically so that each retains its chemical identity.

model
A physical or symbolic representation or simulation of a *system being studied.

modularity
A pattern of repeated components which are interchangeable.

module *See* photovoltaic module.

moisture content
The mass of the moisture in a material relative to the dry mass of the material, expressed as a percent.

molecule
A *chemical combination of two or more *atoms.

monitoring
Observation and evaluation of conditions over time.

monitoring well
A well for collecting water samples in order to measure *water quality, *groundwater level, or the presence and concentration of *contaminants.

monoculture
The planting of a single crop over a large area.

monomer
A simple *molecule that can be bonded to similar molecules to form a *polymer.

monsoon
A seasonal reversal in surface *winds and *precipitation caused by large-scale differential heating of land and ocean surfaces.

Montreal Protocol
An international treaty signed in 1987 which phases out the production and use of *ozone-depleting *chlorofluorocarbons.

moral standing
The status of an entity whose interests matter intrinsically and must be given consideration in the moral assessment of actions and events.

morbidity
The rate of occurrence of a disease.

mortality
The rate of death within a *population.

mosaic
A variegated pattern of different *land uses and *habitat types across a *landscape, none of which is dominant enough to be connected to others. *See also* landscape ecology; patch.

mottling
The presence of spots or streaks of different *soil colors, typically in poorly drained soil.

mountaintop removal *See* mining, mountaintop removal.

MRF *See* material recovery facility.

MRL *See* maximum residue limits.

MRT *See* mean radiant temperature.

MSDS *See* material safety data sheet.

MSW *See* municipal solid waste.

Mt *See* megaton.

muck
An organic *soil consisting of highly *decomposed organic material.

mulch
A layer of organic material spread over the surface of *soil.

multi-attribute
1 Referring to a standard which captures a number of environmental or *life cycle *attributes or impacts.
2 Referring to a structured process for decision-making which identifies alternatives and ranks them according to preferred attributes.

multidisciplinary
Drawing on the knowledge and methods from two or more fields of study without integrating their alternative perspectives. *Compare* interdisciplinary.

multilateral environmental agreement (MEA)
A treaty, convention, or *protocol between multiple states regarding action on specified *environmental problems.

multiple chemical sensitivity
A syndrome involving allergy-like reactions to even low levels of many kinds of irritants or *toxicants at levels that are generally tolerated by most people.

multi-scale
A process or study which includes two or more levels of organization.

multiway boulevard
A larger-scale *complete street, with spacious sidewalks, tree canopy, and faster traffic lanes physically separated from local access, bicycle, and pedestrian routes.

municipal solid waste (MSW)

Waste from households, offices, institutions, and small businesses; called "municipal" because such waste is the responsibility of local governments.

mutagen

A substance which damages genetic material, or DNA, in cells.

mutation

A change in the DNA sequence of a cell.

mutualism

A relationship between two *species in which both species benefit.

M&V *See* measurement and verification.

MVOCs *See* microbiological volatile organic compounds.

MW *See* megawatt.

mycelium

A network of *hyphae which makes up the body of a *fungus.

mycorrhizae

A *symbiotic relationship between the roots of most plants and certain *fungi.

N

N-11 *See* Next Eleven.

nacelle
The housing for the major components of a ⋆wind turbine including the ⋆generator and gearbox.

naphtha
Generic term for a ⋆petroleum product derived from ⋆fractionation.

NAPL *See* non-aqueous phase liquid.

National Environmental Policy Act (NEPA)
A US law enacted in 1970 which requires ⋆environmental impact statements for federal projects and actions.

National Pollutant Discharge Elimination System (NPDES)
A provision of the US Clean Water Act which prohibits ⋆pollutant discharges from ⋆point sources into water unless authorized by an NPDES permit.

National Priorities List (NPL)
The ⋆EPA's list of the most serious uncontrolled or abandoned ⋆hazardous waste sites identified for possible long-term remedial action under ⋆Superfund.

native species
Species that developed in the place where they live and are adapted to conditions there. *See also* indigenous.

natural
Existing in a state not caused or made by humans.

natural attenuation *See* intrinsic remediation.

natural capital
Environmental resources and ⋆ecosystem services that make all ⋆economic activity possible.

natural gas
A gaseous ⋆fossil fuel formed from fossilized marine ⋆plankton and composed mostly of ⋆methane.

naturalized
Referring to an ⋆introduced species which becomes established in a region and able to flourish without human intervention. *Compare* native.

natural play environment
A play area intended to give children direct connection with nature and composed of plants, stone, wood, and other natural materials.

natural resource
A substance or *energy source found in nature and valuable to humans, such as minerals, plants, or animals.

Natural Step *See* The Natural Step.

natural swimming pool
A recreational *pool in which water is cleansed using *constructed wetlands.

natural ventilation
The use of building design and physical principles of temperature and pressure to move air through interior spaces.

nature
The phenomena of the physical world; although nature includes humans, the term is often used to refer to features and processes separate from human activity.

nature deficit disorder
An informal term coined to describe the impacts of a lack of connection with *nature in children.

nature play *See* natural play environment.

NADW *See* North Atlantic Deep Water.

negative feedback *See* feedback.

negawatt
A *megawatt of *power saved by increasing *efficiency or reducing *consumption.

neoclassical economics
An economic theory which assumes that markets have an inherent logic subject to *supply and *demand and that markets always choose the optimal alternative.

NEPA *See* National Environmental Policy Act.

nest predation
The action of predators who eat juvenile birds in the nest.

net benefit
The difference between total costs and total benefits.

net energy balance
The difference between the *energy produced and energy required to produce it. *Compare* energy returned on energy invested.

net metering
A billing arrangement that allows customers who generate their own *electricity to sell excess electricity to the local power *utility. *See also* group net metering.

net present value
The present *discounted value of a stream of net benefits.

net primary productivity
The rate at which *energy or *biomass has accumulated in an *ecosystem in excess of the energy used for *respiration.

network
A set of nodes and the connections between them.

net zero
A net-zero energy building is one which produces as much energy as it uses over the course of a year.

neurotoxin
A *toxicant that attacks neurons.

neutron
An electrically neutral subatomic particle present in the nuclei of most *atoms.

New Urbanism
An urban design movement similar to *smart growth promoted by the Congress for the New Urbanism.

Next Eleven (N-11)

Large developing economies including Mexico, Indonesia, South Korea,
Turkey, and seven others that along
with the *BRIC countries have a
high potential of becoming the world's
largest economies by the end of the
century.

nexus

A *system or group linked by a connection or series of connections.

NGO *See* nongovernmental organization.

niche

The role an organism plays in its
*ecosystem.

night flushing *See* night ventilation.

night ventilation

A method of *passive cooling that
flushes heat accumulated during the
day and draws in cool outside air at
night.

NIMBY

Acronym for "not in my back yard."
A phenomenon in which residents
oppose something with negative impact
near where they live, even though they
may want it to exist elsewhere.

nitric oxide (NO)

A *nitrogen oxide gas produced during
the burning of *fossil fuels; a component of *photochemical smog.

nitrification *See* nitrogen fixation.

nitrogen

An element that makes up 78% of the
*atmosphere and is an essential nutri-
ent for plant growth.

nitrogen cycle

The movement of *nitrogen in different
chemical forms from the *environment,

to organisms, and then back to the
*environment. *See also* biogeochemical
cycle.

nitrogen dioxide (NO₂)

A *nitrogen oxide gas produced during
the burning of *fossil fuels; a component of *photochemical smog and
*acid rain.

nitrogen fixation

A process in which lightning and some
types of *bacteria break the atomic
bonds in *molecules of *nitrogen, N_2,
converting it to a form that is usable by
plants. *Compare* denitrification.

nitrogen oxides

A group of gases composed of *nitrogen
and *oxygen, including nitric oxide, NO,
*nitrogen dioxide, NO_2, and *nitrous
oxide, N_2O. Known informally as "NOx."

nitrous oxide (N₂O)

A *greenhouse gas with 300 times the
*global warming potential of *carbon
dioxide, emitted by *bacteria, *agriculture, and *fossil fuel *combustion.

NMVOCs *See* non-methane volatile
organic compounds.

noise pollution

Sound that is unwanted or disturbing
to humans or wildlife.

nominal group process

A *group process for generating and
evaluating ideas which allots times for
working individually and times for working as a group.

non-aqueous phase liquid (NAPL)

An *immiscible liquid.

nonbiodegradable

A substance that cannot be broken
down in the *environment by *natural
processes. *Compare* biodegradable.

nonconventional pollutants

A group of water *pollutants not already identified as a *conventional or *priority pollutant; includes color, salt, and *heat.

nongovernmental organization (NGO)

An *organization which is independent of both private industry and government; typically nonprofit.

nonlinearity

A condition in which no simple proportional relationship exists between cause and effect.

non-methane volatile organic compounds (NMVOCs)

*Organic compounds other than *methane that participate in *atmospheric *photochemical reactions.

non-native species *See* exotic species.

nonpoint source

A diffuse source of *pollutants that cannot be tied to a specific point of origin.

nonprofit organization

An *organization whose primary objective is something other than returning a profit to owners or shareholders and whose revenue is directed toward achieving its purpose or mission.

nonrenewable resource

A *natural resource with a finite supply that cannot be replaced once used, or one that cannot be replaced as fast as it is consumed.

nontoxic

Not able to cause injury, illness, or damage through ingestion, inhalation, or absorption. *Compare* toxic.

normalized data

Data expressed as a ratio.

North Atlantic Deep Water (NADW)

The deep portion of the *thermohaline circulation in the North Atlantic Ocean.

North Atlantic Oscillation (NAO)

An irregular climate oscillation in the North Atlantic Ocean involving large-scale changes in ocean surface temperatures and winds. *See also* El Niño/Southern Oscillation.

no-till farming

An approach to growing crops by planting in undisturbed soil covered by crop residues and other mulch. Also known as conservation tillage.

novel ecosystem

A self-organizing *ecosystem composed of *species and their interactions that differ from those that prevailed historically, resulting from human influence.

NOx

Informal name for any of the *nitrogen oxides.

noxious weed

A plant *species designated by a government body as injurious to public health, *agriculture, recreation, *wildlife, or property.

NPDES *See* National Pollutant Discharge Elimination System.

NPL *See* National Priorities List.

nuclear energy

Energy released when the nuclei of uranium *atoms split in the process of *fission or *fusion. *See also* nuclear power plant.

nuclear fuel
A substance whose *energy is stored in its atomic nuclei used as *fuel in *nuclear power plants to produce heat.

nuclear power plant
A *thermoelectric power plant which uses nuclear *fission to generate *heat for producing steam, driving a *turbine to generate *electricity.

nutrient
Any substance taken in by organisms required for growth.

nutrient cycle *See* biogeochemical cycle.

nutrient loading
The quantity of *nutrients entering an *ecosystem in a given period of time.

O

objective
A specific statement of measurable outcomes to be achieved within a stated time period. *See also* goal; mission statement; strategy; vision.

obligate
Requiring a specific *environment to grow.

Occam's razor
A principle of economy in explanation which says that given competing explanations, the simplest one is preferable to the more complex. Also known as the principle of parsimony.

occupancy sensor
A device that detects the presence or absence of people within a space and turns off *lights or equipment when the space is unoccupied.

ocean conveyor belt *See* thermohaline circulation.

ocean current energy
A potential method for generating *electricity using *turbines placed within the currents of the *thermohaline circulation. *See also* tidal energy; wave energy; ocean thermal energy conversion.

ocean thermal energy conversion (OTEC)
A potential method for generating *electricity using *temperature differences between surface and deep waters to drive a *Stirling engine. *See also* tidal energy; wave energy; ocean current energy.

OECD *See* Organization for Economic Cooperation and Development.

off-gassing
The emission of *volatile organic compounds from *synthetic and *natural products.

offset
A voluntary payment made to reduce *pollution or *emissions at one location in order to compensate for an equal quantity of pollution or emissions at another location. *See also* carbon credit.

Ogallala Aquifer
The largest *aquifer in North America which underlies the Great Plains.

O horizon
The top layer of soil above the *A horizon in some soil profiles and consisting of organic matter. *See also* soil horizon.

oil

A liquid *fossil fuel formed from fossilized marine *plankton subjected to geologic *heat and pressure over a long period of time. Also known as *petroleum. *See also* crude oil.

oil recovery

The removal of oil from an oil well.

oil sands *See* tar sands.

oil shale

An underground formation of fine-grained sedimentary rock that contains *kerogen, a waxy *hydrocarbon that can be converted to a heavy oil called *shale oil when heated.

oil spill

An accidental or intentional discharge of *petroleum which reaches bodies of water.

oldfield

An abandoned agricultural field, usually one that was once tilled.

old-growth forest

A *forest consisting of trees of mixed ages including mature trees, *snags, and fallen limbs and trees, with no visible indications of human *disturbance of ecological processes.

O&M *See* operations and maintenance.

on-demand hot water system *See* tankless water heater.

OPEC *See* Organization of Petroleum Exporting Countries.

open access resource

A good or service over which no property rights are recognized, accessible to all.

open graded

*Aggregate all of which is within the same size range.

open-loop recycling

A *cradle-to-grave *recycling process in which material from one product is converted to a new product with a change in material properties. Also known as *downcycling.

open pit mining *See* mining, open pit.

open space

Any land accessible to the public not covered by buildings, built structures, or paving; usually refers to land with *vegetation.

open system

A *system in which *matter and *energy can flow in and out.

operable window

A window that can be opened and closed manually by ordinary users.

operations and maintenance (O&M)

Routine, preventive, scheduled, and unscheduled activities necessary for a building and its systems and equipment to perform their intended function.

opportunity cost

The benefits forgone by undertaking one activity instead of another.

ore

Unprocessed *mineral from which *metals can be extracted.

organic agriculture

The general method of growing crops using environmentally healthy methods and without using synthetic *fertilizers or *pesticides; also known as organic farming.

organic compound

A *molecule containing *carbon atoms; often contains *hydrogen and other *elements as well.

organic farming *See* organic agriculture.

organic fertilizer
Organic material applied to crops as a source of plant *nutrients. *See also* compost; crop residue; green manure; manure.

organicism
The philosophy that all *matter, both animate and inanimate, constitutes a single organic whole. *Compare* animism; pantheism.

organic waste
*Biodegradable material in the *waste stream that is of biological origin.

organization
A group of individuals or entities with a specified common objective; an administrative and functional structure and the people who make up the structure.

Organization for Economic Cooperation and Development (OECD)
An international *organization of governments of developed countries focused on economic and social *development.

Organization of Petroleum Exporting Countries (OPEC)
A group of states organized for the purpose of negotiating with *oil companies on questions of production, prices, and future concession rights.

organopónico
A small-scale *organic urban farm in Cuba or other Latin American countries.

orientation
The position of a building or structure in relation to the sun or compass directions.

oscillating water column (OWC)
Technology for generating *electricity using ocean wave action; rising and falling water in an enclosed chamber compresses air in the chamber, driving a *turbine.

osmosis
The tendency of a *fluid to move across a semipermeable *membrane from a less concentrated solution into a more concentrated one, thus equalizing the *concentrations on each side of the membrane. *See also* reverse osmosis.

OTEC *See* ocean thermal energy conversion.

outfall
The place where *effluent discharges from a point source into receiving waters.

outwash
*Sand and *gravel deposited by meltwater flowing from a *glacier.

overburden
Surface material to be removed that is overlying the material to be mined. Also known as mine spoils. *Compare* tailings.

overconsumption
The act of consuming something in excess of its ability to be renewed.

overdraft
The pumping of water from a *groundwater source in excess of its ability to be recharged, resulting in the groundwater being depleted.

overexploitation *See* overconsumption.

overfishing
Taking more fish from a *fishery than can be replenished within time scales that are relevant for humans.

overgrazing
Feeding by too many grazing animals on an area of *rangeland, resulting in destruction of *vegetation, *compacted soil, and disruption of *ecosystem function.

overharvesting *See* overconsumption.

overland flow
The flow of water over the ground surface when precipitation or snowmelt exceeds the soil's infiltration capacity. Also known as *surface runoff.

overlay
A process in which two or maps, each of which shows specific data, are superimposed to form a composite map which shows all the data and the relationships between features.

overshoot
The gap between the demand for *ecosystem services and the rate at which nature can provide them, that is, the amount by which resource *consumption and *waste production exceed nature's capacity to create new resources and absorb waste.

overstory *See* canopy.

OWC *See* oscillating water column.

oxbow
An abandoned segment of a river channel which forms a crescent-shaped lake, pond, or *marsh.

oxidize
To chemically transform a substance by combining it with *oxygen.

oxygen
A highly reactive gaseous *element with eight *protons, eight *neutrons,

and eight *electrons; present in the *atmosphere, given off in *photosynthesis, and consumed in *respiration.

Oxygenation Catastrophe *See* Great Oxidation Event.

ozone
A gas composed of three *oxygen *atoms bonded together, found in the *ozone layer of the stratosphere and as *ground-level ozone at the bottom of the *troposphere.

ozone, ground-level
A *secondary air pollutant and *greenhouse gas formed in a *chemical reaction between *nitrogen oxides and *volatile organic compounds in the presence of sunlight. A component of *photochemical smog.

ozone, stratospheric *See* ozone layer.

ozone-depleting substance
Any substance that accelerates the destruction of stratospheric ozone in Earth's protective *ozone layer; includes *chlorofluorocarbons and *hydrochlorofluorocarbons.

ozone hole
A seasonal thinning of stratospheric ozone above Antarctica. *See also* Montreal Protocol; ozone layer.

ozone layer
A layer of *ozone which shields organisms on Earth from incoming *ultraviolet radiation, formed when *solar radiation strikes *oxygen molecules in the *stratosphere.

P

Pacific Garbage Patch *See* Great Pacific Garbage Patch.

paleoclimate
Earth's *climate during periods before the development of measuring instruments, including historic and geologic time, for which only *proxy climate records are available.

paleosols
Ancient *soils that have been incorporated into the geological record; paleosols provide information about *paleoclimates.

palustrine wetland
A wetland that is not dependent on streams, lakes, or ocean water.

palynology
The study of pollen, spores, and some microscopic plankton in both living and fossil form.

panarchy
The nested hierarchy of *adaptive cycles at multiple *scales in a *social-ecological system.

panel *See* photovoltaic panel.

pantheism
The philosophy that everything that exists constitutes a unity and that this all-inclusive unity is divine. *Compare* animism; organicism.

parabolic trough
*Concentrating solar technology which uses parabola-shaped mirrors to concentrate sunlight on a linear heat collection tube.

paradigm
A fundamental framework for understanding the world; a coherent set of assumptions and concepts that defines a way of viewing reality. *See also* dominant paradigm.

Paris Agreement
The *UN Framework Convention on Climate Change which replaced the *Kyoto Protocol in 2015.

participation *See* public participation.

particulate material
*Matter in the form of fine solid particles or liquid droplets small enough to be suspended in air or water.

parts per billion (ppb)

The number of parts of a *chemical found in one billion parts of a particular gas, liquid, or solid mixture.

parts per million (ppm)

The number of parts of a *chemical found in one million parts of a particular gas, liquid, or solid mixture.

passenger miles

The total distance traveled by all passengers via air, highway, and light and heavy rail; calculated by multiplying the occupancy rate in vehicles by the *vehicle miles traveled.

passenger modes

Methods of transporting people including private vehicles and *public transit. *Compare* freight modes.

passenger rail

Methods of transporting people including commuter rail, light rail, heavy rail, and subway.

passive cooling

Methods for removing *heat from a building which uses *natural ventilation.

PassivHaus

A European design standard for energy-efficient buildings that use *passive heating and cooling methods.

passive solar heating

Methods for using sunlight for heating without the use of active mechanical devices such as pumps or fans.

passive ventilation

Methods for using air movement for cooling without the use of active mechanical devices such as pumps or fans. *See also* natural ventilation.

pastoralism

A livelihood strategy based on moving livestock to seasonal pastures primarily in order to convert plants or plant residues into human food.

patch

A discrete *habitat area large enough to support breeding by a particular *species.

pathogen

An organism capable of causing diseases in humans, animals, plants, or other organisms.

pathway

The physical route by which a chemical substance transfers from a source to exposed organisms. *See also* transport.

payback period

The time required to recover the cost of an investment through subsequent savings.

PBT *See* persistent, bioaccumulative, and toxic.

PCB *See* polychlorinated biphenyl.

PE *See* polyethylene.

peak demand *See* peak load.

peak discharge

The maximum rate of flow in a *stream for a given condition, such as a storm event or snowmelt; measured in cubic meters per second or cubic feet per second.

peak load

The maximum *electricity demand for a building or *utility over a given time interval. Also known as peak demand or peak power. *Compare* base load.

peak oil
The point at which *oil reaches its highest production levels, after which the rate of production declines.

peak phosphorus
The point at which *phosphorus extracted from *phosphate rock reaches its highest production levels, after which the rate of production declines.

peat
Partially decomposed plant material that has accumulated in a water-saturated *anaerobic environment.

peer review
The process in which writing or research work is evaluated by outside experts in a relevant field to determine whether the work is of high enough quality to publish.

pelagic zone
Water of the open ocean or lakes, between the surface and the bottom.

pellet *See* wood pellet.

penstock
1 A large pipe for conveying water to a *hydroelectric *turbine.
2 A gate or sluice for regulating the flow of water.

people, planet, profit
An alternative term used in the business world to describe the *triple bottom line.

perched water
A zone of *groundwater which sits above the *water table.

percolation
The downward movement of water through the *soil, primarily due to of gravity.

percolation rate
The rate at which water moves into *soil through the walls of a test pit.

perennial stream
A *stream that flows continuously in parts of its bed year-round. *See also* baseflow. *Compare* ephemeral stream; intermittent stream.

perfluorocarbons (PFCs)
A group of *chemical *compounds containing carbon and fluorine only, introduced as alternatives to *ozone-depleting substances; powerful *greenhouse gases with high *global warming potentials.

permaculture
A design strategy for *agriculture and human *communities based on observing patterns in nature; the word was coined by combining the words "permanent" and "agriculture."

permafrost
Underground *soil or rock that remains frozen year-round. *See also* tundra.

permeability
The rate at which water can move through *soil. *Compare* porosity.

permeable paving
A paving material that allows water to *infiltrate the *soil.

permit trading *See* emissions trading.

persistence
The property of a substance which lasts a long time without changing.

persistent, bioaccumulative, and toxic (PBT)
A class of *pollutants that are resistant to degradation, that accumulate in organisms, and that are *toxic; includes

*dioxin, *phthalates, *lead, and *mercury compounds.

persistent organic pollutant (POP)

A class of organic *chemicals that remain unchanged for long periods of time, accumulate in the food chain, and are *toxic to humans and other animals.

perturbation *See* disturbance.

perverse subsidy

A tax benefit or payment from government which makes environmentally harmful activities more economically feasible. *See also* subsidy.

pervious paving *See* permeable paving.

pest

An unwanted organism perceived to have negative impact on health, human economic interests, or the *environment.

pesticide

A *synthetic substance designed to kill unwanted organisms; categories of pesticides include *insecticides, rodenticides, *herbicides, and *fungicides.

PET *See* polyethylene terephthalate.

petrochemical

A *chemical obtained by refining *crude oil or *natural gas.

petrochemical feedstock

*Feedstock derived from *petroleum and used in the manufacture of *chemicals, *synthetic rubber, and *plastics.

petroleum

One of the three types of *fossil fuel; also known as *oil.

PFCs *See* perfluorocarbons.

pH

A scale which indicates the degree of *acidity or *alkalinity, based on a measure of the *concentration of *hydrogen *ions in water.

phantom power

*Energy consumed by *electronic devices when they are turned off or in standby mode. Also known as energy vampires.

phenology

The study of the relationship between seasonal changes, *climate, and recurring biological phenomena such as flowering, breeding, and *migration.

phosphate rock

The unprocessed *mineral from which *phosphorus is extracted.

phosphorus

An *element with 15 *protons, 15 *neutrons, and 15 *electrons; involved with transferring and using *energy within *cells and a key *nutrient for plant growth. *See also* phosphate rock.

phosphorus cycle

The *biogeochemical cycling of *phosphorus through the *rock cycle, *hydrosphere, and *biosphere.

photochemical smog

*Secondary air pollutants formed when *nitrogen oxides and *volatile organic compounds chemically react with sunlight.

photoelectric effect

The phenomenon in which light is converted directly to *electric current; when photoelectric material is hit by sunlight, *electrons are ejected from one side and emitted from the opposite side.

photosimulation *See* simulation.

photosynthesis
The process by which green plants and other *autotrophs synthesize carbohydrates from *carbon dioxide and water using sunlight as an *energy source. *Compare* respiration.

photovoltaic (PV)
Technology that that converts sunlight directly into *electricity using *semiconductor materials.

photovoltaic array
An assembly of connected *photovoltaic panels fastened to a supporting structure.

photovoltaic cell
A *semiconductor device which converts *solar energy directly to *electricity.

photovoltaic effect *See* photoelectric effect.

photovoltaic module
A group of connected *photovoltaic cells.

photovoltaic panel
A group of connected *photovoltaic modules in a supporting frame.

phthalates
A group of *chemicals widely used as *plastic softeners in toys and other *plastics and as fragrance-enhancers in cosmetics; phthalates are *carcinogens and *endocrine disruptors.

phytoplankton
Microscopic, single-celled *photosynthetic organisms including *cyanobacteria, *diatoms, and *algae that live suspended in water and form the base of the marine *food web.

phytoremediation
The use of plants to treat *pollutants.

phytostabilization
The use of plants to keep *contaminants from moving through soils.

pioneer
A *species that colonizes a site in the earliest stages of *succession.

pipeline
A line of pipe with pumping machinery and apparatus for conveying liquids, gases, or finely divided solids between distant points.

pisé
Soil mixed with *cement and used in *rammed-earth construction.

place-based learning
An approach to learning in which curriculum is based on local knowledge. *See also* bioregionalism.

plan-do-check-act cycle
A four-step quality management approach that involves an ongoing cycle. Also known as the Deming Cycle. *See also* continuous improvement.

planetary boundaries
A framework of nine interdependent conditions which define a safe operating space for maintaining a stable, *Holocene-like state within which humanity can continue to develop and thrive into the long-term future. The boundaries are *climate change, *biodiversity loss, excess *nitrogen and *phosphorus production, stratospheric *ozone depletion, ocean acidification, freshwater consumption, *land-use change, *air pollution, and chemical *pollution.

plankton
*Microorganisms that live suspended in water. *See also* phytoplankton; zooplankton.

planning
The processes of using scientific, technical, and other knowledge to provide choices for decision-making and the processes for considering and reaching consensus on alternative options. *See also* land use planning; regional planning; urban planning.

plantation
A large area of land on which primarily a single crop is grown. *See also* monoculture.

plastic
A *synthetic *polymer, typically made from *petroleum.

plasticity
The property of a solid material which irreversibly deforms under stress without breaking, such as in the convection currents in Earth's upper *mantle or in the yielding of a metal which has been stressed beyond its elastic limit.

plasticizer
An additive that softens and increases the pliability of a *polymer.

plate tectonics
The process by which large sections of *crust or tectonic plates move very slowly across Earth's surface because of *convection currents in the *mantle. *See also* continental drift.

Pleistocene epoch
The geological *epoch during which the most recent *ice ages occurred, extending from about 2.6 million years ago to the beginning of the *Holocene epoch.

Pleistocene rewilding
An approach to ecological *restoration which proposes the reintroduction of *proxies for *megafauna who were once native to a region in order to fill the *niches they once occupied.

plug-in hybrid electric vehicle (PHEV)
A *hybrid vehicle that can use *electricity from its batteries but which has the option to get *power from a gasoline engine. *Compare* battery-electric vehicle.

plume
A visible or measurable mass of a *contaminant from a given point of origin.

PM$_{2.5}$
*Particulate matter which is less than or equal to 2.5 micrometers in diameter.

PM$_{10}$
*Particulate matter which is less than or equal to 10 micrometers in diameter.

POE *See* post-occupancy evaluation.

point source
A source of *pollution that comes from a single, identifiable source.

poison *See* toxicant.

polar cell
A large-scale circulation of air through the entire depth of the *troposphere near the poles, with air flowing toward the equator near the surface and poleward at higher altitudes. *Compare* Ferrel cell; Hadley cell.

policy
Formalized principles by which a government or *organization is guided. *See also* public policy.

pollinator
An insect or other animal that transfers pollen from one flower or part of

a flower to another, fertilizing the plant and allowing it to make fruit or seeds.

pollutant
A substance with adverse effects on the health of living organisms; a substance that makes up *pollution.

polluter pays principle
The principle that an entity causing *pollution should pay the costs of reducing that pollution and the costs of damage caused by the pollution. *Compare* user pays principle.

pollution
The presence or accumulation of substances with adverse effects on the health of living organisms. *See also* air pollution; water pollution; pollutant.

pollution prevention
The design of a process or activity to reduce or eliminate the creation of *pollution or *waste at the source.

polycarbonate
A strong *plastic used to manufacture products including food packaging, containers, DVDs, and *glazing; sometimes contains bisphenol-A. Can be labeled with a number 7 *resin identification code.

polycentric governance
A *governance system with participation and interaction by a diverse array of *communities and public and private authorities with overlapping domains of responsibility and operating at multiple scales.

polychlorinated biphenyl (PCB)
A class of *persistent organic pollutants formerly used as coolants and lubricants in *electrical equipment, now banned but still *bioaccumulating in *food webs worldwide.

polyculture
The growing of two or more crops in a given area at the same time. *See also* intercropping.

polyester
A group of *polymers which can be *thermoplastics or *thermosets; commonly used in textiles. *See also* polyethylene terephthalate (PET).

polyethylene (PE)
A *thermoplastic *polymer. *See also* high-density polyethylene; low-density polyethylene.

polyethylene terephthalate (PET)
Also abbreviated PETE. A type of *polyester used in the manufacture of food and beverage containers. Its *resin identification code is 1.

polymers
Complex molecules formed by long chains of *monomers, such as proteins, *cellulose, and *synthetic *plastic.

polypropylene (PP)
A *polymer used in a range of applications including toys, textiles, and containers. Its *resin identification code is 5.

polystyrene (PS)
A tough *polymer used in packaging, containers, and disposable cutlery. Its *resin identification code is 6. Often used in its foamed state when it is known as *expanded polystyrene.

polyurethane
A tough, rubber-like, usually *thermosetting *polymer used in carpet pads, seals, hoses, and protective coatings. Used in its foamed state as an insulating material on roofs.

polyvinyl chloride (PVC)
A *polymer used in water piping and many consumer products; hazardous

when burned. Also known as vinyl. Its *resin identification code is 3.

pond
A body of standing water small enough that sunlight can reach the bottom across the entire diameter.

pool
1 A relatively deep *stream *habitat with relatively slow water velocity.
2 A location where matter in a *biogeochemical cycle is stored. *See also* reservoir.

POP *See* persistent organic pollutant.

population
A group of individuals of one *species living within a particular area.

population density
The number of individuals in a given *population per unit area.

population ecology
The study of the growth, decline, and changes in *populations of organisms.

porosity
A measure of the volume of open spaces in *soil or rock. *Compare* permeability.

porous asphalt
A paving mix which uses *open-graded angular *aggregate but is otherwise identical to conventional asphalt paving.

porous block pavement system
A prefabricated paving material made of concrete or plastic formed in lattice structures, designed to support light vehicle traffic and pedestrians while allowing *stormwater *infiltration and the growth of *vegetation.

porous concrete
A paving mix which uses *open-graded *aggregate but is otherwise identical to conventional concrete.

porous paving
A paving system which includes a *permeable surface underlain by an excavated reservoir filled with *open-graded *aggregate to detain and cleanse *stormwater and to allow *infiltration and *recharge.

Portland cement
A *cement made by burning ground limestone and clay and used in structural *concrete.

positive feedback *See* feedback.

post-consumer waste
Materials generated by a business or *consumer and recovered for *reuse or *recycling after having served their original purpose.

post hoc fallacy
A logical fallacy that if two variables occur in succession, one causes the other; short for the Latin phrase *post hoc ergo propter hoc*: "after this, therefore because of this."

post-industrial waste
Materials generated in a *manufacturing process and recovered for *reuse or *recycling.

post-occupancy evaluation (POE)
A systematic process of evaluating building performance after it has been occupied based on occupant feedback and quantitative measurement.

potable water
Water which is suitable for human consumption.

potential energy
The stored *energy of position.

poverty
The pronounced deprivation of *well-being.

power
The rate at which *energy is transferred.

power conditioning unit
A component of a *photovoltaic system which helps optimize electrical output and includes the *inverter, overload protection, and disconnect.

power grid See grid.

power plant
A facility containing *prime movers, electric *generators, and auxiliary equipment for converting *mechanical, *chemical, *solar, *thermal, and/or *nuclear energy into *electric energy.

power tower
A type of *concentrating solar power technology composed of multiple *heliostats that focus sunlight on a receiver at the top of a centrally located tower.

PP See polypropylene.

ppb See parts per billion.

ppm See parts per million.

prairie
An *ecosystem in flat or rolling *topography dominated by grasses and low-growing flowering plants.

precautionary principle
An approach to making decisions in a way that leaves a margin of safety because of the possibility of causing unexpected harm.

precession of the equinoxes
*Changes in the direction of Earth's axis of rotation on a 26,000-year cycle. See also Milankovitch cycles.

precipitation
*Condensed moisture from the *atmosphere that falls to Earth as rain, hail, snow, sleet, dew, or frost.

pre-consumer content
Materials generated in a *manufacturing process and recovered for *recycling prior to *consumer use.

precycling
The practice of reducing *waste by avoiding the use of items that generate waste.

prediction
The act of attempting to produce a description of the expected future. Compare projection; scenario. See also forecast.

preemergent
A type of *herbicide applied to *soil to prevent *weed seeds from germinating or emerging.

prescribed burning
The practice of deliberately setting and controlling fires in *forest or *grassland to affect *ecosystem composition or to help prevent catastrophic fires.

present value
The value of a future cost or benefit assessed in terms of its present *economic value. See also discounting.

preservation
Efforts to maintain an area in a state that is relatively undisturbed by humans.

preservative
A substance added to a product with the primary purpose of inhibiting the growth of *microorganisms.

primary consumer
An organism that eats *autotrophs or plants; also known as an herbivore.

primary energy
Energy embodied in *natural resources that has not undergone conversion by humans to other forms.

primary forest *See* old-growth forest.

primary pollutant
A *pollutant released directly into the air from its source, already formed. *Compare* secondary pollutant.

primary production
The accumulation of *energy by plants through *photosynthesis. *See also* net primary productivity.

primary source
In research, an original source of information including direct evidence, direct observation, and first-hand accounts.

primary treatment
The first stage of *wastewater treatment which removes floating and suspended solids.

prime mover
A device, such as an engine or motor, that converts *energy from some source into *mechanical energy to provide motion.

priority pollutant
One of a group of *water pollutants listed by the *EPA and *EEA as *hazardous substances of particular concern.

probability
A quantitative measure of the likelihood of a particular outcome. *See also* statistics.

process map
A graphic method of mapping workflow in an *organization using adhesive notes, flowcharts, or simple sketches.

procurement
The process of acquiring products and services including establishing requirements, evaluating vendors, negotiating contracts, and actual *purchasing.

produced water
*Wastewater that comes to the surface with *oil, created when water is injected into oil and gas reservoirs to force oil to surface. *Compare* drilling fluid.

producer *See* autotroph.

producer gas *See* synthetic gas.

producer responsibility *See* extended producer responsibility.

productivity
A measure of efficiency.
1 (economics) The rate of production; the quantity of output per unit of input.
2 (biology) The rate at which *biomass is produced by an *ecosystem. *See also* net primary productivity.

product life cycle *See* life cycle.

product takeback *See* takeback.

project
A one-time task with definite starting and ending points and clearly defined *scope of work.

projection
The act of attempting to produce a description of the future, subject to assumptions about certain preconditions. *Compare* prediction. *See also* forecast.

prokaryote
A single-celled organism that lacks a nucleus. *Compare* eukaryote. *See also* Archaea; bacteria.

protist
One of a group of mostly single-celled organisms with nuclei; includes protozoa, single-celled algae, and slime molds.

protocol
The methods, rules, and procedures to be followed.

proton
A positively charged particle within the nucleus of an *atom.

provisioning services
The products obtained from *ecosystems including food, water, and fiber. *See also* ecosystem services.

proxy
An *indicator which stands in for another measurement.

PS *See* polystyrene.

psychrometric chart
A graph used by building designers which shows the relationships of temperature and moisture in air.

publication
In scholarship, a *peer-reviewed paper which communicates methodology and findings to a larger audience.

public domain
Property rights that belong to the community at large, such as land owned by a government or works of art, writing, or music not subject to copyright or patent protection.

public good
A good or service from which it is difficult to exclude or limit users and in which use of the resource by one person does not decrease the benefits for others. *Compare* common pool resource.

public participation
The process of people working together to define their own objectives and find

their own solutions and the ability of those people to influence decisions.

public policy
Policy that is made by and enforceable by governments.

public transportation
*Transit modes in which multiple people travel in the same vehicle; includes bus, *bus rapid transit, and *light rail. Also known as mass transit.

Public Utility Regulatory Policies Act (PURPA)
US law allowing *independent power producers to connect their *generators to a utility-owned *grid and requiring *utilities to purchase that produced *power at a just and reasonable price.

pulp
A slurry from which paper and cardboard are *manufactured, produced by chemically or mechanically separating *cellulose fiber from *recycled paper, wood, *hemp, grasses, or other plants.

pump-and-treat
A method of treating contaminated *groundwater by pumping it to the surface, treating it to remove *pollutants, and returning it underground.

pumped storage
*Hydroelectric power generation using water which is pumped to an upper storage *reservoir during off-peak periods, then released to drive *turbines during *peak-demand periods.

purchasing
The process of ordering, receiving, and paying for goods and services. *See also* procurement.

PURPA *See* Public Utility Regulatory Policies Act.

purple pipe
The color of plumbing pipe tradition-ally used for ★graywater.

PV *See* photovoltaic.

PVC *See* polyvinyl chloride.

pyranometer
An instrument for measuring the ★albedo of a material.

pyrolysis
A process of heating ★biomass at moderately high ★temperature in the absence of ★oxygen. *See also* biochar; charcoal.

Q

qanat
An underground, gravity-fed water-supply tunnel transporting water from an *aquifer in a foothill and accessed by vertical shafts; originally developed in Persia.

quad
One quadrillion *Btus.

qualitative
Relating to non-quantitative characteristics or attributes.

quantitative
Relating to numerical data.

quarry
An *open-pit mine from which *sand, *gravel, and stone are extracted.

Quaternary Period
The most recent geological period in Earth's history extending from about 2.6 million years ago to the present; includes the *Pleistocene, *Holocene, and *Anthropocene epochs.

R

radiant cooling
A strategy in which cold water circulates through tubes in a *chilled beam or a floor *slab, transferring heat out of a space by *radiation.

radiant heat *See* radiation.

radiation
1 Energy emitted in the form of *electromagnetic waves.
2 The transfer of heat energy through matter or space by electromagnetic waves emitted by a body. *Compare* conduction; convection.

radiative forcing
A change in *solar irradiance caused by variations in climate factors, such as changes in *greenhouse gas concentration or variations in Earth's orbit.

radioactive decay
The process in which the unstable nucleus of an *isotope emits high-energy subatomic particles, changing it to another isotope or to a different *element.

radioactive waste
Any *waste that emits *energy as rays, waves, or streams of energetic particles.

radioactivity
The emission of subatomic particles as unstable atomic nuclei decay.

radon
A naturally occurring radioactive gas formed in the *radioactive decay of *uranium.

rail freight
The movement of freight between cities by trains.

rail transportation
A passenger or freight transportation mode in which vehicles with steel wheels roll on steel rails or tracks which determine their travel path. *See also* light rail.

rain barn
An open-air shed with a large roof area constructed for the purpose of catching rainwater.

rain barrel
A small tank that collects and stores rainwater from roofs. *See also* cistern; rainwater harvesting.

rain chain
A device made of chain used as an alternative to a downspout to guide runoff from a roof and to minimize splash.

rain garden
A planted depression in the landscape where *stormwater runoff collects temporarily as it *infiltrates into the soil below.

rainfall intensity
The amount of rain falling in a given time period, expressed as inches or mm of rainfall depth per hour.

rainforest *See* tropical rainforest.

rainwater endowment
The amount of rainwater which can be captured on a particular site.

rainwater harvesting
The process of collecting water that falls as rain and storing it for later use.

rammed earth
A construction method in which *soil is laid in formwork and compacted in layers. See also *pisé*.

rangeland
Land covered with grass or long-term forage growth whose plants provide food for grazing animals. *See also* grassland.

reach
A segment of a stream between tributaries or between two points marked by a change in valley and channel form, *vegetation, *land use, or ownership.

reactivity
The tendency of a substance to undergo a *chemical reaction with another substance.

reactor core
The part of a nuclear reactor in which *fission occurs.

rebound effect
A phenomenon in which greater efficiency in one area is offset by greater

consumption elsewhere. *See also* Jevons' paradox.

REC *See* renewable energy certificate.

receiver
A component of a *solar energy facility that receives solar energy and converts it to useful *energy forms, typically *heat.

receiving water
A water body into which *stormwater, *wastewater, or treated *effluent discharges.

recharge
The replenishment of *groundwater with water which *infiltrates from the surface.

recharge zone
An area where water can *infiltrate the *soil and eventually reach *groundwater.

reclaimed
A material which is processed for reuse but not significantly altered.

reclamation
The process of restoring a degraded site to an ecologically healthy state.

reconciliation ecology
An approach to *restoration that deliberately shares the places where humans live with other *species.

recovery
The diversion of materials from the *municipal solid waste stream for the purpose of *recycling or *composting.

recyclable
A product or material *recovered from the *solid waste stream which can be processed and transformed into materials for the *manufacture of other products.

recyclate
Material to be *recycled.

recycled
Materials that have been previously processed and are reused to *manufacture the same or a different product.

recycled content
The proportion of a material by weight that is composed of materials recovered from the *waste stream, including *recycled, *pre-consumer, and *post-consumer waste.

recycling
A *waste disposal method which extracts materials from the *waste stream and processes them so that they can be reused in some way.

recycling coordinator
A person employed by an *organization to set up, manage, monitor, and provide training for a *recycling program.

recycling rate
The ratio of total *waste *recycled to total waste generated.

red bag waste
Medical waste, handled separately from other *waste because it can contain *pathogens.

redlining
The practice of denying services to a particular neighborhood based on its racial or ethnic composition.

Red List of Threatened Species
A global catalog of *species facing risks of *extinction, maintained by the International Union for Conservation of Nature and Natural Resources (IUCN).

reductionism
The belief that complex phenomena can be understood by analyzing their individual parts. *Compare* complexity.

redundancy
The presence of more than one *system element with similar function so that one can compensate for another.

reference site
A functioning *ecosystem chosen to serve as a model for planning a *restoration project, with characteristics that the impaired ecosystem is expected to emulate when it is restored. *See also* baseline.

refinery
An industrial facility that converts *crude oil into finished *petroleum products. *See also* fractionation.

reflectance
The ratio of the amount of *light striking a surface to the amount of light leaving the surface.

reforestation
The planting of *forests on lands that have previously contained forests but that have been converted to some other use.

reformer
A device used to extract *hydrogen from *natural gas or other *hydrocarbons.

refrigerant
A working *fluid used in refrigeration cycles because of its ability to absorb or give off heat when it changes phase. *See also* heat pump.

refugium
An area of relatively unaltered *climate or other *ecosystem conditions that is inhabited by a *species or *community of species during a period of *extinction in surrounding areas, and from which new dispersal and speciation may take place in the future.

refuse
Any *waste materials rejected as unable to be reprocessed or *reused. *See also* solid waste.

regenerative

Relating to an approach that not only reverses damage but that improves and enhances *ecosystem health. *Compare* restoration.

regime

The characteristic pattern and set of states in which a *system can exist and still retain its basic structure and function.

regime shift

A large and persistent change in the structure and function of a *system in which it crosses a *threshold from one relatively stable state to another.

region

A broad geographical area with a common *climate and sphere of human activities; smaller than a continent and larger than a *landscape.

regional planning

*Planning which deals with *land use, development patterns, growth, and environmental protection in a broad geographical area or a *bioregion at a scale larger than *urban planning.

regulating services

The services that *ecosystems provide in the regulation of processes, such as regulating *climate or moderating extreme weather events. *See also* ecosystem services.

regulation

A rule issued as a means to carry out legislation, usually enforced by a regulatory agency.

rehabilitation

The improvement of *ecosystem processes and functions without returning the site to pre-existing conditions.

reintroduction

The release of animals into an area where they existed in the past. *See also* captive breeding; introduction.

relative humidity

The ratio of the amount of moisture in the air relative to the amount it could hold at that *temperature, expressed as a percentage; technically, the ratio of the vapor pressure of water vapor in the air relative to the vapor pressure of the air when it is saturated.

relocalization

A strategy for rebuilding local *communities based on the local production of food, *energy, and goods and guided by local *governance and culture.

remanufacturing

The process of repairing or rebuilding products or parts in order to use them again with the same function.

remediation

The process of cleaning up a *polluted site using physical, chemical, or biological means.

remote sensing

The science of obtaining information about Earth's surface from a distance using instruments mounted on aircraft or satellites.

renewable energy

Energy, usually *electricity, produced by *energy sources that are continually replenished including *wind, *solar energy, *hydropower, *geothermal energy, and *biomass.

renewable energy certificate (REC)

A tradable commodity that represents a unit of *electricity generated from a *renewable energy source; also known as renewable energy credits, green certificates, or green tags.

renewable resource

A resource that is replenished by natural processes and not depleted by moderate use.

replacement fertility rate

The number of births per woman that will maintain the human *population size constant at zero population growth. *See also* birth rate; fertility rate.

reproductive health

1 A state of physical, mental, and social well-being in all matters relating to the reproductive system.

2 A field of health services which includes family planning, maternal health, child health, prevention of sexually transmitted diseases, and prevention of gender-based violence.

reserve

1 (ecology) A protected area set aside for *conservation of particular *species or *habitats.

2 (fossil fuels) The total known amount of an economically recoverable resource.

reserves-to-production ratio

An indicator of the remaining lifespan of a resource, usually *fossil fuel, calculated by dividing the total remaining *reserves by the amount produced per year.

reservoir

A location where *energy or *matter are stored in *systems.

residence time

The average amount of time that a substance spends in a particular *reservoir.

residential

A building sector that consists of structures used primarily as *dwellings for one or more households each, with more than 50% of *floorspace used for residential activities. *Compare* commercial.

resilience

The capacity of a *system to accommodate change and still retain the same function and structure.

resin

A natural or *synthetic *polymer used as the basis of *plastics, adhesives, varnishes, and other products.

resin identification code

A number placed within a triangular logo and imprinted on some *plastic products to indicate the type of plastic from which the item is made.

resource

The total quantity of a material that exists in the Earth's *crust, whether or not it has been discovered.

resource depletion

The consumption of a *resource faster than the rate at which it can regenerate.

resource recovery

The extraction and use of materials or *energy from the *waste stream.

respiration

The *metabolic process by which organisms convert *oxygen and *biomass to *carbon dioxide, releasing *energy. *Compare* photosynthesis.

restoration

Activity to assist the recovery of degraded *biodiversity and *ecosystem function in a particular area.

restoration ecology

A scientific discipline that focuses on the recovery of degraded *biodiversity and *ecosystem function.

retention basin

A *pond or depression containing a permanent *pool for temporarily storing *stormwater runoff to allow *infiltration and to reduce the peak rate of flow. *See also* detention basin.

retrocommissioning

The *commissioning of an existing building to compare its actual operation to its intended design potential.

return on investment (ROI)
The calculation of profit or loss relative to *capital invested.

reusable
A material or product that can be used again without reprocessing its constituent materials.

reuse
The use of a product more than once in its same form without reprocessing.

revalorization
Getting new value from an existing material or product through *reuse or reprocessing.

revegetation
The establishment of plants on *disturbed land by seeding, transplanting, or *natural plant colonization.

reverse osmosis
A water treatment process in which water under pressure is pushed through a *membrane. *See also* osmosis.

rewilding
The restoration of large-scale *habitat through the *reintroduction of large predators as *keystone species.

rhizosphere
The area of *soil immediately around plant roots.

R horizon
The deepest layer of soil in a *soil profile. Also known as regolith or bedrock. *See also* soil horizon.

riffle
A relatively shallow segment of *stream *channel characterized by rapid and at least somewhat turbulent flow.

right-of-way
A strip or area of land granted for any use other than the owner's personal use, often for highways or *utilities.

rill
A small channel formed by soil *erosion during *surface runoff.

Rio Declaration
A set of 27 principles agreed to at the *Earth Summit in Rio de Janeiro in 1992.

Rio Earth Summit *See* Earth Summit, Rio.

Rio + 20 *See* UN Conference on Sustainable Development.

riparian
Relating to or inhabiting the banks of a stream or *river.

riprap
A layer of large rock or broken concrete placed against a slope to prevent *erosion by water.

risk
The *probability of an adverse consequence due to the presence of a *hazard.

risk assessment
A qualitative or quantitative evaluation of the *risks associated with a product, process, or activity.

risk factor
A characteristic or variable associated with increased *probability of an adverse effect.

risk management
The process of considering information from *risk assessment, weighing alternatives, and selecting appropriate prevention and control measures.

river
A large *stream.

robustness
The capacity of a *system to perform without failure across a range of conditions.

rock

Any coherent, naturally occurring substance composed of *minerals.

rock cycle

The large, slow cycle by which rock is created, altered, and destroyed through tectonic, weathering, metamorphic, and igneous processes.

ROI *See* return on investment.

roll-off bin

An open-top metal trash receptacle carried directly on truck frames, rolled off and onto the ground at a job site; larger than a *dumpster.

roof garden *See* intensive green roof.

roof pond

A type of *indirect gain system in which water is located on a roof, protected by movable *insulation, where it radiates *heat into or out of an interior space for *passive heating or cooling.

route of exposure *See* pathway.

rule of 70

An approximate formula for calculating doubling time by dividing the number 70 by the percent growth rate.

rule of capture

A landowner's legal right to capture *groundwater, *runoff, *oil, or gas with no duty of care to other landowners; the first person to capture a *natural resource owns that resource.

runoff

Water from *precipitation or *irrigation that is not *evaporated, *infiltrated, or *transpired and that flows across the land surface rather than within a defined channel. *See also* stormwater runoff.

runoff coefficient

A number given to a type of ground surface representing the percentage of rainfall converted to overland flow and expressed as a number between 0 and 1.

run-of-river

A *hydroelectric power configuration that channels a portion of a river's flow through a canal or pipe without significantly disrupting the flow of river water.

R-value

A measure of a material's resistance to *heat flow.

S

safe
A condition under which the *probability of *risk is extremely low.

safe harbor agreement
A voluntary agreement allowing landowners to degrade a *habitat in some ways in exchange for contributing to the recovery of *threatened or *endangered species in other ways.

safe operating space *See* planetary boundaries.

salinity
The salt content or saltiness of water, usually measured in parts per thousand by mass.

salinization
The buildup of salts in *soils.

saltwater intrusion
The movement of saltwater into *freshwater *aquifers.

salvage
The recovery of *reusable materials from buildings or products.

salvage logging
The practice of removing economically valuable dead trees following a wildfire or other *disturbance. Also known as post-fire logging.

sand
Mineral particles 0.05 to 2.0 mm in diameter. *See also* soil texture.

sanitary landfill
A *landfill engineered to prevent leaks from contaminating *soil and water.

sanitary sewer
A system of underground pipes that carry *wastewater. *Compare* storm sewer.

savanna
A biome found in dry tropical regions characterized by *grassland and isolated trees.

scale
1 A spatial, temporal, quantitative, or analytical dimension used to measure the relative extent or resolution of objects or phenomena.
2 The relationship between a distance on a map, drawing, or photograph and the actual physical distance.

scarify
1 To break up the soil surface to improve conditions for seed germination or planting.

2 To cut or scratch the hard seed coat to aid germination.

scenario
A plausible description of how the future might develop based on assumptions about key driving forces. *Compare* forecasting; prediction.

scenario planning
A structured *planning approach built on plausible, evidence-based, what-if stories about the future.

scenic integrity
A measure of the degree of intactness and wholeness of the *landscape character; the absence of visual disturbance.

scenic quality
A measure of the intrinsic beauty of landform, water form, or *vegetation in the *landscape, as well as any visible human additions or alterations to the landscape.

scenic value
The importance of a *landscape based on human perception of its *scenic quality.

science
The systematic observation of the physical world and its phenomena in order to gain a deeper understanding of physical reality and its governing principles.

scientific consensus
The collective position and opinion generally agreed upon at a given time by most scientists specialized in a particular field of study.

scientific method
A systematic study of a problem in which scientists, collectively and over time, observe and describe a phenomenon, develop a hypothesis, collect data, and use the data to evaluate the hypothesis.

scope
A definition of the work to be done, the functional unit, and the system boundaries.

scope creep
The phenomenon in which a *project continues to expand beyond its original boundaries while planning or the project itself is underway.

scraper *See* grazer.

scrubber
An *air pollution control device that uses a liquid or *slurry spray to remove *pollutants from *flue gases.

sea ice
Ice found at the surface of the ocean that has formed by the freezing of seawater.

sea-level rise
A change in the elevation of global *mean sea level resulting from the *thermal expansion of warming ocean water or the melting of land-based *ice sheets.

seat-mile
A unit of measure in aviation equal to one commercial airline seat flown one mile.

secondary forest *See* second-growth forest.

secondary pollutant
An air *pollutant formed as a result of *chemical reactions between *primary pollutants and other constituents in the air.

secondary source
In research, a source of information that presents and interprets information gained from *primary sources.

secondary treatment

The second stage of *wastewater treatment in which *aerobic bacteria degrade organic material and suspended solids are then removed by settling.

second-growth forest

A *forest that has regrown in a previously forested area following a major *disturbance such as logging or fire; younger than and lacking the *structural diversity of an *old-growth forest.

second-party certification

An assessment against a standard by an *organization which has an interest in the entity being certified and which is not the producer of the standard. *Compare* third-party certification.

sector

In *energy analysis, a broad category denoting a type of energy *consumer or *greenhouse gas emitter: *residential, *commercial, *industrial, or *transportation.

sediment

Particles which originate from the *weathering and *erosion of *rock and are *transported by, *suspended in, or deposited by water or air.

sedimentation

The *deposition of *sediment particles into a body of water.

sedimentation basin

A *pond or depression used to allow *sediment in water to settle out; may be part of a *detention or *retention facility.

sediment deposition *See* deposition.

sediment fence

A temporary barrier used in construction consisting of filter fabric stretched across support posts to detain *sediments in *runoff. Also known as a silt fence.

sediment transport

The movement of *eroded *soil particles in flowing water.

seed bank

1   The reserves of viable seeds present in soils.
2   Seeds stored by humans for farming or to preserve genetic *diversity.

segmentation

The process of subdividing human *populations into groups based upon social, cultural, or other attributes. *See also* social marketing.

self-organization

The ability of a system to structure itself or to create new structure. *See also* emergence.

semantic vagueness

The characteristic of a word whose meaning is unclear and indefinite.

semiarid climate

A *climate with 10 to 20 inches of *precipitation per year.

semiconductor

A material that conducts *electric current under some conditions and whose electrical properties can be manipulated.

sensible heat

*Heat that can be felt or sensed and can be measured with a thermometer. *Compare* latent heat.

septic system

A system that treats and disposes of household *wastewater in an underground *septic tank and drain field.

septic tank
An underground tank for *wastewater treatment by *anaerobic bacteria.

sequestration *See* carbon sequestration.

service learning
Learning by doing while working on solutions to *community problems.

servicizing
An invented word which refers to the practice of providing a service instead of a product.

setback
The distance of a structure or other feature from the property boundary.

sewage
*Residential or *industrial *wastewater discharged into *sewers or *septic systems.

sewage lagoon
A method of *wastewater treatment in which *sewage flows into three *lagoons for *primary, *secondary, and *tertiary treatment.

sewage sludge
A semi-solid residue separated during *wastewater treatment. Becomes *biosolids when treated for *pollutant and *pathogen removal.

sewage treatment *See* wastewater treatment.

sewer
An underground pipe or conduit that carries *stormwater or *wastewater. *See also* sanitary sewer; storm sewer.

sewer access
An underground chamber that allows maintenance access to *sewers and other *infrastructure. Also known as a manhole.

sex ratio
The proportion of males to females in a *population.

shading coefficient
The ratio of *solar energy transmitted by *glazing compared to a single pane of clear glass. *See also* solar heat gain coefficient.

shadow flicker
The flickering effect that occurs when a *wind turbine casts shadows over structures and observers at times of day when the turbine rotor is between the observer and the sun.

shale gas
*Natural gas trapped within shale deposits; generally extracted by *hydraulic fracturing.

shale oil
A slow-flowing, heavy *oil produced when *kerogen in *oil shale is heated; subsequently refined to produce *gasoline and other *petroleum products.

sharing economy
An *economic model based on sharing, trading, or renting of products and services, reducing levels of individual ownership of goods; can be person-to-person or business-to-consumer. Also known as collaborative consumption.

sheet piles
A type of *pollutant *containment consisting of sheets of steel driven into the ground.

shellac
A protective coating for wood, made from *resin exuded by lac insects found in India and Southeast Asia.

shelterbelt *See* windbreak.

SHGC *See* solar heat gain coefficient.

short-circuiting
In a *constructed wetland or *sewage lagoon, the flow of water through part of a basin faster than intended.

short ton
2000 pounds; equal to 0.907 *metric tons.

shredder
1 An animal in an aquatic *food web who feeds on leaf litter or other coarse particles of organic matter. *Compare* collector; grazer.
2 A machine used to break *waste materials into smaller pieces to minimize volume or to facilitate *incineration.

shrubland
A region with hot, dry summers and *vegetation dominated by shrubs, such as *chaparral and *savanna.

sick building syndrome
A condition in which occupants of a building experience symptoms while in the building but in which no specific cause can be identified. *Compare* building-related illness.

sidelighting
*Daylighting in which sunlight comes in through windows in a vertical wall.

silica
Silicon dioxide, a naturally occurring mineral in sand and stone; silica dust is *hazardous when inhaled.

silicon
A common *element found in *silica sand and a *semiconductor used to *manufacture computer components and *solar cells.

silo
An insulated, vertical unit within an *organization with little outside exchange of information.

silt
Soil with particles 0.05 to 0.002 mm in diameter. *See also* soil texture.

silviculture
The management of *forests for the production of timber.

silvopasture
The integration of pasture understory for livestock with trees or other woody plants. *Compare* agroforestry.

single-stream recycling
A method of recycling *municipal solid waste in which all material considered *recyclable is collected together. Also known as commingled recycling.

sink
A *reservoir where matter is stored and removed from *system interactions. *See also* carbon sink.

sinuosity
A measure of the amount of curvature in a *stream channel, given by stream length divided by valley length between two points.

SIP *See* structural insulated panel.

sisal
A coarse, stiff fiber produced by the leaves of a species of agave plant found in Mexico and Central America; used to make twine, brush bristles, floor mats, and other products.

skylight
A *glazed opening in a roof or ceiling used as a type of *toplighting.

slab cooling
A type of *radiant cooling in which cool air or chilled water is circulated through a *concrete floor slab.

slag
The mostly nonmetallic by-product left after metals are *smelted from *ore.

slash
Woody debris that remains after the logging of trees.

slash-and-burn agriculture *See* swidden agriculture.

slope
The incline of a land surface, usually expressed as a percentage.

SLOSS debate
Single large or several small (SLOSS), a debate in *ecology and *conservation biology during the 1970s and 1980s over whether it was better to make reserves large in size and few in number or many in number but small in size. *See also* fragmentation; island biogeography; landscape ecology.

slough
An elongated *swamp or shallow lake, often adjacent to a *river or *stream.

sludge
A semi-solid residue of municipal or *industrial water or *wastewater treatment. *See also* sewage sludge.

sludge, activated *See* activated sludge.

sludge, industrial
A semi-liquid residue left after the treatment of *industrial water or *wastewater.

slurry
A free-flowing suspension of insoluble matter in a liquid.

slurry wall
A type of *pollutant *containment built by digging deep trenches and filling them with a nonpermeable material such as *bentonite clay or a mixture of *clay and *soil.

smart grid
A networked *microgrid that uses two-way meters, intelligent controls, telecommunications, and distributed storage to distribute *electricity. *See also* microgrid; distributed generation.

smart growth
An approach to *urban planning which features compact, *walkable, and *transit-oriented neighborhoods with a mix of uses, housing types, and affordability levels.

smart infrastructure
A system of sensors, controls, and user interfaces embedded in *infrastructure and the equipment it interacts with, with the ability to respond to environmental changes and to influence and direct its own use.

smart meter
A two-way gas or *electric meter that communicates consumption rates to a *utility and sends price signals to users.

smelting
A process of extracting metal from *ore by heating and melting.

smog
Short for *photochemical smog, *secondary air pollution formed by the interaction of *pollutants and sunlight.

smog, industrial
Gray-colored *photochemical smog which forms in industrial areas without strong sunlight. Also known as gray air.

snag
A standing, dead tree or a standing section of tree trunk.

Snowball Earth
A period 750 to 580 million years ago during which positive *feedback caused the planet to be almost entirely covered by ice.

snow pack
Horizontal layers of accumulated snow.

social capital
The capacity of a society to act in a cohesive way, built upon its cultural institutions and relationships. *See also* capital.

social change
A change in activity within *communities, cultural, or political institutions. *Compare* behavior change; structural change.

social diffusion
The diffusion of change or innovation in which an idea or behavior spreads through social contacts. Also known as the diffusion of innovation.

social-ecological system
A linked *system of humans and *nature.

social insect
A type of insect such as ants, bees, or termites who are members of cooperative communities known as *superorganisms in which *complex behaviors emerge out of their interactions as a *community rather than from individual decision-making.

social justice
The fair distribution of resources and opportunities to all people.

social marketing
The use of marketing techniques to achieve specific *behavioral changes to improve social *well-being.

soil
A complex *ecosystem of mineral particles, organic matter, air, water, and living organisms.

soil horizon
One layer of *soil in a *soil profile.

soil moisture
Water held in the unsaturated zone of soil. Also known as green water.

soil profile
The pattern of *soil layers in a particular place from the surface toward the *bedrock below.

soil protection plan
Part of a set of construction documents with instructions for preventing loss of *topsoil and soil *compaction on a construction site.

soil stabilizer
A *chemical that alters the structural properties of a natural *soil; used to stabilize slopes and prevent *erosion.

soil stack
A vertical pipe, or stack, that carries *blackwater.

soil texture
The percentage by weight of *sand, *silt, and *clay-sized particles in a *soil.

soil vapor extraction
A *soil *pollution *treatment method in which volatile components of *petroleum are extracted from air in wells and then removed by filtering through *activated carbon.

solar array *See* photovoltaic array.

solar cell *See* photovoltaic cell.

solar chimney
A tall duct that heats up when exposed to sunlight to enhance the *stack effect.

solar collector
A device that converts *solar energy to *thermal energy, used as a *solar water heater or as part of a *concentrating solar power facility.

solar cooker
A simple portable oven that uses reflectors to focus sunlight to heat and cook food.

solar dish See dish concentrator.

solar energy
Direct radiant energy from the sun.

solar garden
A *community solar array with multiple subscribers connected to the *utility grid. See also group net metering.

solar heat gain coefficient (SHGC)
A measure of the percentage of *solar radiation that passes through a window, expressed as a value from 0 to 1.

solar heating See passive solar heating; solar hot water.

solar hot water See solar water heater.

solar intensity See solar irradiance.

solar irradiance
A measure of solar *power; the amount of *solar radiation received per area perpendicular to incoming radiation, expressed in *watts per square meter.

solarium See sun space.

solar module See photovoltaic module.

solar orientation
The position of a building or structure in relation to the sun. See also orientation.

solar panel See photovoltaic panel; solar water heater.

solar photovoltaic See photovoltaic.

solar radiation
Electromagnetic energy emitted by the sun.

solar reflectance See albedo.

solar reflectance index (SRI)
A measure of a material's *temperature in the sun; a composite of solar reflectance or *albedo and *emittance, expressed as a percentage or as a value from 0 to 1.

solar thermal energy
The use of *heat from the sun to heat *domestic water or to create steam in a *concentrating solar power system.

solar tube See light pipe.

solar water heater
A system in which *solar energy is absorbed by *collectors to produce *domestic hot water. See also evacuated tube collector; flat plate collector.

solid waste
Garbage, refuse, *sludge from water, *wastewater, or *air pollution treatment; *waste from industrial, commercial, mining, and agricultural operations and from community activities; does not include *sewage, *irrigation residue, *point source *effluent, or *nuclear waste.

solvent
A substance capable of dissolving another substance to make a new solution.

soot
Particulate matter consisting primarily of carbon emitted as a result of incomplete *combustion. Also known as *black carbon.

sorption
The physical or chemical process in which a substance is attracted to the surface of a solid. *See also* absorption; adsorption.

source
A storage compartment in the *environment that releases matter to another location.

source reduction
The reduction in the quantity of material used through design of products and packaging, decreased *consumption, or *waste prevention.

source separation
The segregation of recyclable materials by type at the point of discard.

SOx
Informal name for *sulfur dioxide (SO₂).

space heating
The use of an individual item of mechanical equipment to heat all or part of an interior space.

sparging
The injection of air directly into *groundwater to increase *oxygen available to *bacteria. *Compare* venting.

specialist
A *species that can survive only in a narrow range of *habitats or that can feed on only one or a few species. *Compare* generalist.

speciation
The evolution of a new *species from an existing species.

species
A group of organisms with physical and genetic similarity, able to breed with one another and produce fertile offspring.

species diversity
The number of *species within a given region and the relative abundance of each species.

species richness
The number of *species in a given community or area.

spectrally selective coating
A type of *low-emissivity coating that is transparent to visible sunlight but that reflects *infrared heat.

spent fuel
*Nuclear fuel that has been used in a reactor to the extent that it can no longer effectively sustain a chain reaction.

spent materials
Materials that have been used and can no longer serve the purpose for which they were produced without processing.

spoil
*Waste *soil or rock left after *mining, dredging, or excavation.

sprawl
A human settlement pattern characterized by low-density *land use, single-use *zoning, and automobile dependency.

spring
A location where a *water table meets the *soil surface or where *groundwater emerges onto the surface.

square foot gardening
A form of *biointensive agriculture where the planting bed is divided into one-foot squares with a single crop planted in each square.

SRI *See* solar reflectance index.

stack
A vertical pipe or chimney that discharges air.

stack effect
The tendency of air to become buoyant and rise when heated. *See also* passive cooling.

stack ventilation
A method of using *natural ventilation for cooling in which rising *heat in a building creates a *stack effect.

staging area
A designated location where construction equipment is temporarily stored during a construction project.

stakeholder
A person or group who can be impacted by an outcome or decision.

standard deviation
In *statistics, a measure of how spread out or close a set of numbers is to the mean, given by the square root of the variance.

standard of living
The ease with which people in a particular *population are able to satisfy their wants; often based on average *gross domestic product per capita.

state
The values of the set of attributes or variables that characterize a *system at a particular time.

stationary source
A source that is fixed in space.

statistics
The mathematics of the collection, organization, and interpretation of numerical data, often to draw conclusions about a larger set of data based on a representative sample.

steady state
The condition in which inputs and outputs of a *system are in *equilibrium.

steam field
An area where steam is extracted from deep within the earth for the purpose of providing *geothermal energy.

steppe
An *ecoregion with a *semiarid climate and *vegetation consisting of grasses and low-growing plants.

stepping stone
One of a series of disconnected *habitat patches within a *matrix that can function as a *corridor for migration and dispersal of some *species.

stewardship
Responsible care of the *natural world. Also, the belief that humans have a unique responsibility to make decisions about the use and management of *natural resources.

Stirling engine
A *heat engine that operates at low pressures using a *temperature difference between a hot source and a cold sink to drive pistons as gas inside heats and cools.

stock
An accumulation of material or information that has built up in a *system over time.

Stockholm Convention
An international treaty signed in 2001 which limits or eliminates the production of persistent organic *pollutants.

storage, hydroelectric power *See* pumped storage.

storm sewer
A system of underground pipes that carry *stormwater. *Compare* sanitary sewer.

storm surge
A temporary rise in local sea level due to low *atmospheric pressure or strong

winds above the level expected from tidal variation alone.

stormwater
Water that falls as rain.

stormwater runoff
Water from precipitation that flows over surfaces into *sewer systems or receiving waters. *See also* runoff; stormwater.

stranded asset
Capital or resource, such as *fossil fuel or a water-intensive crop, that has been devalued or become a financial liability prematurely.

strategy
A specific action plan for achieving a *goal. *See also* mission statement; objective; vision.

stratigraphy
The study of rock layers or strata in order to understand geologic history or to establish units of the *geologic time scale. *See also* International Commission on Stratigraphy.

stratosphere
The upper layer of *atmosphere that lies above the *troposphere. *See also* ozone layer.

stratospheric ozone *See* ozone layer.

straw bale
A construction technique in which bales of straw are stacked between structural members, pinned together, and covered by plaster or stucco to provide an insulated wall.

straw mud
A building technique using a material similar to *cob that is pressed between forms and then coated with plaster.

straw poll
An unofficial, nonbinding vote to help gauge support or help bring potential conflicts into the open.

stream
A general term for a body of flowing water. *See also* river.

stream geometry
The shape of a *stream including width, depth, *gradient, and *sinuosity. *See also* fluvial geomorphology.

stream order
A method of classifying the *hierarchy of *stream channels within a *watershed.

stream profile
The change in elevation in a *stream channel over a given distance.

stream terrace
A landform consisting of an abandoned *floodplain.

strip mining *See* mining, strip.

stripper well
An *oil or *natural gas well that produces at declining rates as it nears the end of its economically useful life.

strong sustainability
The *economics concept that human and *natural capital are not interchangeable and that natural capital is the limiting factor.

structural change
A regulatory and policy-based approach to sustainability solutions, in contrast to an individual approach. *Compare* behavior change; social change.

structural complexity *See* structural diversity.

structural diversity
Variation in the vertical and horizontal features of a *landscape.

structural insulated panel (SIP)
A premanufactured panel used in residential and light construction made of a foam core such as *expanded polystyrene

sandwiched between wood sheathing, usually oriented strand board.

structure
1 The physical organization of a *system.
2 A collection of interdependent parts in a definite pattern of organization.

submetering
The practice of using additional *electric meters provided by building owners to record *energy use in selected portions of a facility.

subscription farming
The name given to *community-supported agriculture in Europe.

subsidence
The sinking of a part of the Earth's surface.

subsidy
A direct payment or tax reduction from a government to a private party in order to encourage a particular activity or practice. *See also* perverse subsidy.

subsistence farming
A form of *agriculture in which most output is consumed directly by a household.

subsoil
The layer of soil below the *topsoil or *A horizon. Also known as the *B horizon.

substation
An *electric power distribution facility that includes transformers to change voltage and switchgear to control or disconnect power.

substitutability
The extent to which human-made *capital can be substituted for *natural capital. *Compare* complementarity.

subsurface flow
The movement of water below the ground surface. *See also* groundwater flow.

subsurface-flow wetland
A form of *constructed wetland in which *wastewater flows through gravel below the surface.

subtropics
The parts of the Earth immediately north and south of the *tropics.

suburb
A *residential or *mixed-use area located on the edge of an urban area.

suburban sprawl *See* sprawl.

succession
Progressive change in *species composition, *structure, and *ecosystem characteristics in a *community, often in response to a *disturbance.

sulfur cycle
The movement of sulfur in different chemical forms from the *environment, to organisms, and then back to the environment. *See also* biogeochemical cycle.

sulfur dioxide (SO$_2$)
A *pollutant resulting from the burning of *fossil fuels, particularly *coal; also known informally as *SOx. *See also* acid rain.

sulfur hexafluoride (SF$_6$)
A gas with an extremely high *global warming potential, used in electrical transmission and distribution systems and electronics.

sump
A well or hole in which water is collected.

sun angle
The angle of the sun vertically above the horizon and the *azimuth angle along the horizon from true south.

sun angle chart
A graph used to plot the location of the sun in the sky at various hours of the day and months of the year.

sun space
A glass-walled room designed to collect *heat.

sunspot
A dark area of reduced *temperature that forms temporarily on the surface of the sun in approximately 11-year cycles; causes slight differences in *solar irradiance.

supercluster *See* galaxy supercluster.

Superfund
The program mandated by *CERCLA and operated by the *EPA for *remediation of particularly *polluted sites.

superorganism
A complex, cooperative *community of *social insects.

supply
(economics) The amount of a product available at a given price. *Compare* demand.

supply chain
A network of individuals and *organizations who *procure, process, *manufacture, and distribute materials, components, and services, resulting in a final product.

surface drainage divide *See* drainage divide.

surface impoundment
A natural or human-made depression or diked area used to volatize or settle *hazardous waste.

surface roughness
1   A measure of the diversity of building heights, *vegetation, and topography in an urban area related to *urban heat island mitigation.
2   The height of deviations from an ideal smooth form in a solid surface, such as a machined part.

surface runoff
The flow of water over the ground surface when *precipitation or snowmelt exceeds the *soil's infiltration capacity. Also known as *overland flow.

surface water
Water open to the *atmosphere, such as *rivers, lakes, reservoirs, and *springs.

suspended load
*Sediments that are carried by water in a *stream or *river.

sustain
To endure or maintain over long periods of time.

sustainability
The state in which the needs of all members of the *biosphere are met without compromising the ability of future generations to meet their needs.

sustainability indicator *See* indicator.

sustainability science
An *interdisciplinary field of study of the interactions between natural, social, and human systems and with how those interactions impact *sustainable development.

sustainable agriculture
Farming practices which are economically and socially acceptable and that do not deplete *natural resources faster than they can regenerate.

sustainable development
*Development that meets the needs of the present generation without compromising the ability of future generations to meet their own needs.

Sustainable Development Goals
A set of 17 goals replacing the *Millennium Development Goals, adopted by *United Nations members in 2015 and aimed at ending poverty, supporting *social justice and *economic progress, restoring *ecosystems, promoting *sustainable and *resilient cities, and addressing *climate change.

sustainable forestry
The management of *forests in a way that meets human needs for timber and food while conserving and maintaining the long-term health of forest *ecosystems.

sustainable urbanism
An approach to *urban planning that includes *mixed-use, compact, and *walkable neighborhoods with a range of housing types and connections to nature, served by public *transit corridors, and consisting of *high-performance buildings and *green infrastructure.

sustainable use
A method of using resources or meeting needs in such a way that we can continue to do so indefinitely.

sustainable yield
The extraction level of a *renewable resource which does not exceed its rate of growth or regeneration.

swale
A linear drainage channel with a *vegetated surface. *Compare* gutter. *See also* bioswale.

swamp
A type of *wetland dominated by trees or shrubs.

sweatshop
A shop or factory in which employees work long hours at low wages under unhealthy or inequitable conditions.

swidden
A seminomadic form of *agriculture in which *forests are cleared, crops are cultivated until *soil fertility declines, and then new regions are cleared. Also known as slash-and-burn agriculture.

swimming pool, natural *See* natural swimming pool.

switchgrass
A warm-season perennial grass native to North American tallgrass prairies; can be used as *feedstock for *biofuel.

SWOT analysis
A strategic planning approach for identifying strengths, weaknesses, opportunities, and threats; strengths and weaknesses are internal factors while opportunities and threats are external influences.

symbiosis
A relationship between two organisms from different *species who live with and interact with each other, benefiting both of them.

synergy
A process in which the combined effect of interacting factors is greater than the sum of the separate effects of those factors.

syngas *See* synthesis gas.

synthesis
The combining of separate elements to form a coherent whole.

synthesis gas
A *fuel gas produced through the *gasification of *coal or *biomass. Also known as syngas.

synthetic
A *chemical or substance *manufactured by humans as opposed to one formed by *natural processes.

synthetic fertilizer *See* fertilizer, synthetic.

synthetic natural gas
A *manufactured gas chemically similar to *natural gas, made by converting or *reforming *petroleum *hydrocarbons.

synthetic oil
Liquid *hydrocarbons synthesized from *carbon dioxide, *carbon monoxide, and *methane by the *Fischer-Tropsch process. *Compare* crude oil; fractionation.

system
An integrated whole made of interconnected parts.

systems thinking
A way of perceiving reality which considers relationships, processes, and interconnected parts of unified wholes.

T

tactic
A specific project or action taken in order to implement a strategy.

taiga *See* boreal forest.

tailings
Residue of crushed rock that has been processed during *mining to release a metal of interest. *Compare* overburden.

take-back program
A practice in which manufacturers assume responsibility for *reusing or *recycling the products which they produced.

take–make–waste
An informal name for a linear flow of materials, products, and waste. *Compare* borrow-use-return. *See also* cradle to grave; life cycle.

tankless water heater
A system to produce hot water for domestic purposes which provides hot water only as needed to eliminate standby energy losses. Also known as on-demand water heater, demand-type water heater, and instantaneous water heater.

tank-to-wheels emissions
A *life cycle analysis *scope including *emissions generated by fuel use in vehicles. *Compare* well-to-tank; well-to-wheels.

tar sands
A naturally occurring deposit of *sand impregnated with *bitumen, a *heavy oil that is extracted by *heating; subsequently refined to produce *petroleum products.

task lighting
Lighting that is focused on a specific surface, object, or activity.

tax shifting
A restructuring of tax *policy so that activities which cause harm, such as *pollution, are taxed, while activities which are desired, such as personal income production, are not taxed. *See also* green tax.

TBL *See* triple bottom line.

TDM *See* transportation demand management.

team
A group of people with a shared goal.

technical metabolism
In *cradle-to-cradle systems, the cycle in which *technical nutrients flow. *Compare* biological metabolism.

technical nutrient
A material that will not *biodegrade or become part of any *ecosystem. *See also* cradle to cradle; technical metabolism.

technology
The application of scientific knowledge to the conversion of resources into outputs for the benefit of humans.

TEEB
The Economics of Ecosystems and Biodiversity, a global initiative launched by *UNEP to draw attention to the global economic benefits of biodiversity and to provide a basis for valuation of *ecosystems and *ecosystem services.

TEK *See* traditional ecological knowledge.

temperate zone
The parts of the Earth between the *tropics and the poles; characterized by moderate *temperatures.

temperature
The average *thermal energy of the *molecules in a substance; a measure of heat intensity.

teratogen
A substance which causes abnormalities in developing embryos.

terrace, stream *See* stream terrace.

terracing
The creation of level platforms in steps cut parallel to *contours on a sloping site to minimize *erosion and *runoff and to allow crop cultivation.

terrain
The topographic layout and features of a tract of land. *See also* topography.

terra preta
Fertile, black-colored *soil enhanced with *biochar by pre-Columbian civilizations; found in the Amazon rainforest.

terrestrial
Pertaining to land, as opposed to water.

terrestrial radiation
The total *infrared radiation emitted by the Earth and its *atmosphere; the *radiation emitted by every object.

terroir
The cumulative effect of *environmental factors including *climate, *microclimate, *soil, and *topography on the flavor characteristics of foods.

tertiary treatment
The third and final stage of *wastewater treatment in which inorganic nutrients including *nitrates, *phosphates, and fine particles are removed; may include disinfection. Also known as polishing.

thalweg
The channel within a *stream that carries water during low-flow conditions; a line connecting the points of lowest streambed *elevation.

theory
An explanation of a phenomenon that has been rigorously tested and become accepted by a general consensus of scientists.

therm
A unit of *heat equal to 100,000 *British thermal units.

thermal bridging
The flow of *heat through a conductive element in the building *envelope that bypasses the *insulation system.

thermal capacity
The amount of *heat energy needed to raise the *temperature of a substance one degree, or its capacity to hold heat; proportional to weight. Also known as heat capacity.

thermal chimney *See* solar chimney.

thermal energy
The kinetic energy of *atoms and molecules; also known as *heat.

thermal expansion
The increase in volume of a material as its *temperature increases.

thermal mass
A heavy, dense building material which absorbs *heat, stores it, and reradiates it slowly.

thermal pollution
An unhealthy change in water *temperature.

thermal storage
A storage medium that stores collected *heat for later use, such as tanks in a *concentrating solar power facility or a rock bed in an *isolated gain *solar heating system.

thermal treatment
The treatment of *hazardous waste using elevated *temperatures to change the chemical, physical, or biological character of the waste.

thermodynamics
A branch of physics that deals with the transformation of *energy.

thermodynamics, first law of
The law of conservation of *energy, which states that energy can neither be created nor destroyed.

thermodynamics, second law of
The law of *entropy, which says that *energy tends to change from a more ordered to a less ordered state.

thermoelectric power plant
A facility that uses *heat to create steam which spins *turbines for generating *electrical energy. *See also* power plant.

thermohaline circulation
A global deep-ocean circulation *system driven by *temperature and *salinity. Also known as the global conveyor belt.

thermoplastic
A *synthetic *polymer which melts or remelts upon heating above a specific *temperature. *Compare* thermoset. *See also* plastic.

thermoset
A *synthetic *polymer which melts once but does not remelt upon *heating. *Compare* thermoplastic. *See also* plastic.

thermostat
A device that activates *heating or cooling controls in response to changes in *ambient temperature.

third-party certification
A process in which the body empowered to conduct a *certification audit is independent from the body seeking *certification.

threatened species
A *species considered to be likely to become *endangered in the near future.

Three Mile Island
The site of a US *nuclear power plant in Pennsylvania where nuclear reactors partially melted down in 1979.

three pillars of sustainability *See* triple bottom line.

threshold
A level of variables in a *system at which *feedbacks cause the system to change irreversibly to a new state. *See also* tipping point.

throughput
The amount of materials and *energy that flow through a *system.

tidal energy
A form of *renewable energy generated by differences in ocean water level between low and high tide. *See also* wave energy, ocean current energy, ocean thermal energy conversion.

till *See* glacial till.

time of concentration *See* concentration time.

time value of money
The concept that the present value of money is worth more than its future value. *See also* discounting.

tipping fee
A fee charged for the unloading or dumping of *solid waste at a *landfill, *transfer station, or *incinerator.

tipping point
The critical transition at which accumulated small changes cause a *system to shift abruptly and irreversibly into a new state. *See also* threshold.

TOD *See* transit-oriented development.

tolerance range
The range of a given parameter within which an organism can function.

ton *See* metric ton; short ton.

ton-mile
A measure equal to moving one ton of freight a distance of one mile.

toplighting
*Daylighting in which sunlight comes into a room from above. *See also* atrium; light well; skylight.

topography
The shape of a land surface; the relative positions and *elevations of natural and human-made land features of an area.

topping cycle
A *combined-heat-and-power system in which electricity is the primary product and heat is the secondary product. *See also* bottoming cycle.

topsoil
The uppermost layer of *soil. Also known as the *A horizon.

tornado
A funnel-shaped *cyclonic storm over land extending from a storm cloud toward or in contact with the surface.

total quality management (TQM)
A systematic management approach built on employee participation at all levels, customer focus, fact-based decision-making, and continuous improvement.

total suspended solids
Fine particles suspended in water, too small to be removed by settling.

tower, wind turbine
The base structure that supports and elevates a *wind turbine rotor and *nacelle.

toxic
Able to cause injury, illness, or damage through ingestion, inhalation, or absorption. *Compare* nontoxic.

toxicant
A substance that is harmful to living organisms. *Compare* toxin.

toxicity
The degree to which a substance can damage living cells.

toxicology
The study of the adverse effects of *chemicals on biological systems and the conditions under which those effects occur.

toxin
A *toxicant produced by a living organism.

TQM *See* total quality management.

traceability
The ability to verify the history, application, or location of a material or item through a supply chain. *See also* chain of custody.

tradable permits *See* emissions trading.

trade balance
The difference between the resources used to produce the goods and services exported or their monetary value and the resources used to produce the goods and services imported or their monetary value.

trade-off
A choice that involves losing one benefit or *ecosystem service in return for gaining another.

trade winds
Prevailing easterly winds found in the tropics of the Northern and Southern Hemispheres near the Earth's surface.

traditional agriculture
A method of farming based on local knowledge and local resources, developed through the interaction of social and environmental systems.

traditional biomass *See* biomass, traditional.

traditional ecological knowledge (TEK)
The cumulative, dynamic body of knowledge about the *natural world acquired by *indigenous and local people over time through direct experience and interaction with their local *environment.

tragedy of the commons
The degradation of a public resource; the accumulated result of decisions by multiple self-interested individuals to maximize their own personal interests. *See also* commons.

transboundary pollution
*Pollution that originates in one jurisdiction but is able to cause damage to the *environment in another jurisdiction by crossing borders through *pathways of water or air.

transect
A line established on the ground along which observations are made or data are collected.

transfer station
A facility where *solid waste is collected from smaller vehicles and placed into larger vehicles for transport.

transformation
A change in the fundamental attributes of an existing *system such that a new system is created.

transit
The movement of people or goods from one place to another. *See* public transportation.

transit desert
An urban area in which residents do not have ready access to *public transportation.

transit-oriented development (TOD)

An element of *smart growth in which neighborhood development is clustered around convenient *transit stations and located along transit corridors.

transmission

(energy) The movement or transfer of *electric energy over an interconnected group of lines, support structures, and associated equipment from a *power *generation source to an electric distribution system. *See also* grid.

transmittance

A measure of the amount of *solar radiation that passes through a material, expressed as a percentage.

transnational

A relationship that operates or extends across national boundaries.

transparency

Open, comprehensive, accessible, and understandable disclosure of information.

transpiration

The movement of water through plants.

transport

The ways in which a *pollutant moves through the *environment. *See also* pathway.

transportation demand management (TDM)

A set of tools and strategies for changing travel behavior in order to reduce the number of automobile vehicle trips and *vehicle miles driven.

transportation sector

The *energy-consuming part of the *economy that consists of all vehicles whose primary purpose is transporting people or goods from one physical location to another.

trap

A U-shaped pipe in indoor drainage piping that retains enough water to form a seal, preventing *sewer gases from entering occupied space.

trash audit *See* waste audit.

trawling

A fishing method in which a net or trawl is pulled through the water behind a boat. *See also* bottom trawling.

treatment

Any process that changes a *pollutant or *hazardous waste into a form that is less hazardous or no longer harmful.

treatment, storage, and disposal facility (TSDF)

A site where *hazardous waste is treated, held temporarily, or disposed of.

tree protection plan

Part of a set of construction documents with instructions for preventing soil *compaction or root damage within the *critical root zone of trees on a construction site.

tree protection zone *See* critical root zone.

tree ring

One of several concentric rings of wood each formed during a single period of growth and visible in a cross section of the stem of a woody plant.

triatomic

A *molecule composed of three *atoms.

trickling filter

A *wastewater treatment system in which wastewater trickles over a bed of rocks or other material and *organic waste is broken down by *aerobic bacteria living in *biofilm that covers the bed material.

triple bottom line
The concept that *sustainability rests upon the three pillars of environment, *economics, and *equity, also known as planet, people, profit.

Trombe wall
An *indirect gain *passive solar heating system in which a *thermal mass is located between the interior space and incoming *solar radiation. Also known as a thermal storage wall.

trommel
A rotating cylindrical screen used to separate materials in *solid-waste *resource recovery facilities or *sand and *gravel operations.

trophic level
The position a group of organisms with similar feeding function occupies in a *food web.

tropical dry forest
Deciduous *forest *biome found in tropical and subtropical latitudes where *precipitation is absent during a prolonged period each year. Compare tropical rainforest.

tropical rainforest
*Forest *biome found in warm tropical regions near the equator where *precipitation occurs throughout the year. Compare tropical dry forest.

tropics
The parts of the Earth near the equator which are warm all year because of the direct *sun angle. See also solar irradiance.

tropopause
The boundary between the *troposphere and the *stratosphere.

troposphere
The lowest layer of the *atmosphere, closest to the Earth's surface.

tropospheric ozone See ozone.

true cost
The inclusion of both internal and *external costs in the price of a good or service.

TSDF See treatment, storage, and disposal facility.

tubular skylight See light tube.

tundra
A treeless *biome characteristic of polar and alpine regions, consisting of shrubs and low plants that grow mainly on top of *permafrost.

tung oil
An *oil extracted from tung tree seeds.

turbidity
A measure of water clarity resulting from suspended particles which block *light.

turbine
A device which converts the *kinetic energy of flowing air, water, gas, or steam into rotary mechanical power; used for *generation of *electricity. See also wind turbine.

turning See Great Transition.

typhoon
A *cyclone that occurs in tropical regions of the Pacific Ocean.

U

UGB *See* urban growth boundary.

ultraviolet radiation (UV)
*Electromagnetic radiation with wavelengths shorter than visible *light; most is blocked by the *ozone layer.

umbrella species
A *species, typically with a large home range, for which protecting its *habitat also protects the needs of many other species who share their habitat.

UN *See* United Nations.

uncertainty
An expression of the degree to which a future condition is unknown.

UN Conference on Sustainable Development
A 2012 follow-up conference to the 1992 *Earth Summit which made some progress toward the *Sustainable Development Goals. Also known as Rio + 20.

UN Conference on the Human Environment
The first global environment summit, held in 1972 in Stockholm, Sweden.

unconventional oil
*Petroleum which requires *extraction methods other than conventional vertical drilling due to geologic formations or heavy *viscosity. *Compare* conventional oil. *See also* bitumen; oil shale; shale oil; tar sands.

understory
The layer of *forest *vegetation between the ground and the *canopy.

UNEP *See* United Nations Environment Programme.

UNFCCC *See* United Nations Framework Convention on Climate Change.

United Nations (UN)
An international *organization of member states founded in 1945 to promote peace and human rights and to work collectively in solving international problems of an economic, social, cultural, or humanitarian character and based on the principle of the sovereign equality of all its member states.

United Nations Environment Programme (UNEP)
The UN agency that advocates for the global environment and promotes implementation of the *environmental dimension of *sustainable development.

United Nations Framework Convention on Climate Change (UNFCCC)
The first international climate treaty, adopted in 1992. *See also* Conference of the Parties; Kyoto Protocol; Paris Agreement.

upcycling
A process which converts materials into new materials of higher quality.

upwelling
In the ocean, the rising of cold, nutrient-rich waters from the deep ocean toward the surface. *Compare* downwelling.

uranium
A heavy metallic *element whose *radioactive decay heats the Earth's core; the uranium *isotope U-235 is used in *fission reactions in *nuclear power plants.

urban agriculture
The growing of plants or the raising of animals within and around cities.

urban canyon
City *terrain where a street is lined with tall buildings, creating a pronounced effect on *microclimate including *wind, *temperature, and *air quality.

urban ecology
The scientific study of urban areas as *ecosystems.

urban growth boundary (UGB)
A line adopted by a government body which separates an urban area within which development may occur from surrounding open lands where development is restricted.

urban heat island
The area of relative warmth of a city compared with surrounding rural areas.

urban heat island effect
The phenomenon in which air *temperature in cities is several degrees warmer than in surrounding rural areas.

urbanization
An increase in the proportion of the *population living in urban areas.

urban planning
The professional practice which deals with the *planning of cities.

urban sprawl *See* sprawl.

user pays principle
The principle that the user of a *natural resource should pay the costs of decreasing *natural capital. *Compare* polluter pays principle.

utilitarianism
A theory of *ethics which holds that conduct should be judged by its consequences and that the morally right action is one that produces the greatest good for the greatest number of humans.

utility
1 (energy) An agency or other legal entity that generates, transmits, distributes, or sells *electricity, *natural gas, or water and is subject to governmental regulation.
2 (economics) A measure of satisfaction.

utility-scale
A descriptive term for *power facilities that generate large amounts of *electricity delivered to many users through *transmission and *distribution systems.

UV *See* ultraviolet radiation.

U-value
A measure of a material's ability to conduct *heat; the reciprocal of *R-value.

V

vadose zone
The zone between the land surface and the *water table.

vampire power *See* phantom power.

vegan
A person who eats no animal-derived products and avoids using animals for food, clothing, or other purposes insofar as possible. *Compare* vegetarian.

vegetarian
A person who does not eat meat, poultry, fish, shellfish, or by-products of slaughter; many vegetarians do eat eggs, dairy products, and honey. *Compare* vegan.

vegetation
The plant life or total plant cover in an area.

vehicle-miles traveled (VMT)
The total number of miles traveled by one vehicle in a given period of time; total vehicle-miles is the total distance traveled by all vehicles.

vehicle-to-grid (V2G)
An application in which an *electric vehicle or *plug-in hybrid electric vehicle with excess charge can sell *power back to the *grid.

ventilation
The intentional exchange of indoor air with outdoor air; the circulation of air in a building.

ventilator
A roof-mounted device in which *wind creates pressure on one side to drive air into the space and suction on the other side to draw air out of the space.

venting
*Soil pollution *treatment methods which introduce air under pressure or extract air using a vacuum. *Compare* sparging. *See also* soil vapor extraction.

verification
The systematic practice of independent evaluation of evidence for a particular assertion against agreed-upon or regulatory criteria.

vermiculite
A silicate *clay or mica product expanded by heat to produce a lightweight, porous material capable of holding water and air.

vernacular architecture
Structures built without architects based on local knowledge and traditions, using local materials, and adapted to local climate conditions.

vernal pool
A seasonal or *ephemeral *wetland, typically inundated in winter and spring and dry during summer and fall.

vertical farming
An approach to growing food in vertically stacked layers in controlled indoor environments, often including artificial lighting.

vicious cycle
A series of events reinforced through *positive feedback with an undesirable outcome. *Compare* virtuous cycle.

viewshed
The total *landscape that is visible from a viewing point or travel route.

vinyl *See* polyvinyl chloride.

virgin material
A resource which is being used for the first time in a product; material which has not been through a *recycling process.

virtual water
The quantity of water required for the production of food or other goods, measured at the place where they were actually produced.

virtuous cycle
A series of events reinforced through *positive feedback with a favorable outcome. *Compare* vicious cycle.

viscosity
A measure of a fluid's resistance to shearing force; higher viscosity means higher resistance to flow.

visible light *See* light.

visible transmittance (VT)
A measure of what percentage of the visible spectrum of light is transmitted through *glazing; expressed as a value from 0 to 1.

vision
A clear and compelling image of the ideal future.

visual clutter
The visual interplay of multiple disorganized or unrelated elements resulting in an unpleasant view or a degradation of performance at some task.

visual contrast
The opposition or dissimilarity of various forms, lines, colors, or textures.

visual impact
A change to the visual qualities of a *landscape resulting from *visual contrasts and the human response to that change.

visual resource
Any human-made or *natural object or feature that is visible on a *landscape.

vitrification
The conversion of solids into a glass-like substance through a *heating process; used to stabilize *hazardous wastes by mixing them with molten glass.

VMT *See* vehicle-miles traveled.

VOC *See* volatile organic compound.

volatile organic compound (VOC)
An *organic compound that vaporizes at room *temperature. *See also* microbiological volatile organic compounds; non-methane volatile organic compounds.

volatilization

The transfer of *molecules from a liquid where they are dissolved to the *atmosphere. *Compare* evaporation.

voltage

Potential energy difference; a measure of *energy pushing *electrons through a *conductor.

VT *See* visible transmittance.

V2G *See* vehicle-to-grid.

vulnerability

The sensitivity of people, places, *ecosystems, and *species to harm from exposure to stresses, *disturbances, and shocks. *Compare* resilience.

W

wadi
A channel or valley in *desert regions of Asia and Africa that is dry except during the rainy season.

walkability
A measure of the degree to which daily needs can be met on foot, on routes where walking is safe, pleasant, and easy.

WASCO *See* water service company.

waste
Unwanted or discarded material.

waste audit
An activity in which participants sort and measure the weight of materials in each *waste category. Also known as a trash audit. *See also* recycling rate.

waste diversion
An activity such as *reuse, *recycling, or *composting that treats *waste as a resource and keeps it out of the *waste stream.

waste heat
*Heat produced as an unusable by-product of a process.

waste management
The practice of collecting, transporting, treating, and disposing of *waste.

waste management hierarchy
A framework for minimizing *waste streams in which strategies are prioritized and known as *reduce, *reuse, and *recycle.

waste prevention
Strategies to reduce the amount of *waste generated at the source and to reduce the *hazardous content of that waste through product design, *manufacturing, and *behavior change.

waste stream
The *waste material produced in a region and the paths it follows from its sources to final disposal.

waste-to-energy
A process which captures *methane from *landfills and burns it in gas *turbines to generate *electricity or *heat.

waste treatment
Activities to reduce or eliminate the potential for harm due to *waste.

wastewater
Water that has been used for washing, flushing, *agriculture, or *manufacturing and so contains *waste.

wastewater treatment
The use of mechanical, biological, or chemical processes to modify the quality of *wastewater in order to reduce *pollution levels.

water balance
The ratio of water lost from a *system to water brought into the system.

water bar
A V-shaped trench cut into the surface of a road that collects water and channels it off the road surface to avoid *erosion.

water, blue *See* blue water.

waterborne disease
A disease caused by organisms that live in water.

water budget
1 An accounting of all the water that flows into and out of an area such as a lake, a *wetland, or a *watershed; includes *precipitation, *evapotranspiration, *surface-water flows, *groundwater flows, and human withdrawals and transfers.
2 A calculation of the expected water use of a household based on the type and number of *fixtures, landscape *irrigation needs, and number of occupants.

water closet
A flush toilet.

water conservation
The practice of using less water or using it more efficiently.

water cycle *See* hydrologic cycle.

water-energy nexus
The interconnections between water and *energy including the energy cost of delivering water, the water cost of producing energy, and the interconnected nature of energy and water *infrastructures.

water footprint
The *virtual water content of a good or service.

water pollution
The contamination of water by substances that can cause harm to living organisms.

water quality
The chemical, physical, and biological characteristics of water relative to its suitability for a particular purpose.

water quality standard
A law or regulation that defines the *quantitative and *qualitative water quality *criteria necessary to protect the intended uses of a particular waterbody and places a limit on discharges with the potential to impair the water's quality.

water scarcity
The point at which all the demands on the supply of water or quality of water cannot be met.

water service company (WASCO)
A company which provides water auditing and conservation services for a building and whose fees are paid for out of water-use savings.

watershed
An area of land that drains water to a specific *river system or water body.

water stress
A state in which the demand for water exceeds the available amount during a certain period or when poor quality restricts its use.

water table
The upper boundary of the *groundwater or zone of saturation.

water vapor

Water that is present in the *atmosphere as a gas; an abundant but short-lived *greenhouse gas.

watt

A unit of *power, the rate at which *energy is used or produced. *See also* megawatt.

wattle

Living branches bound together and used to provide protection from *erosion and create a *sediment trap along a streambank. Also known as a fascine.

wave energy *See* oscillating water column. *See also* tidal energy; ocean current energy; ocean thermal energy conversion.

wax

A solid or semisolid material derived from *petroleum distillates or residues, used for surface protection.

weak sustainability

The *economics concept that human-made capital can be substituted for *natural capital.

weather

The short-term variation in *temperature, *precipitation, and wind that occurs day to day.

weathering

Physical, chemical, and biological processes that break down rock into smaller particles. *See also* erosion.

weatherization

Energy efficiency measures for buildings including the improvements to the building *envelope.

wedge approach

A climate *mitigation strategy that divides the total necessary reduction in *greenhouse gas emissions into increments or solution wedges.

weed

A plant considered undesirable or unattractive by humans.

weighting

The act of assignment value-based weighting factors to *criteria based on their perceived relative importance.

weir

A simple hydraulic control structure that regulates the flow of water or measures the rate of discharge.

well-being

A condition in which individuals are able to determine and meet their needs including basic material goods, freedom and choice, health and bodily well-being, good social relations, security, peace of mind, and spiritual experience.

wellhead

The point at which *petroleum or *natural gas exits the ground.

well-to-tank emissions

A *life cycle analysis *scope including *emissions generated by *fossil fuel or alternative fuel extraction, production, and distribution; does not include fuel use in vehicles. *See also* tank-to-wheels; well-to-wheels.

well-to-wheel emissions

*Life cycle analysis applied to *transportation fuels and their use in vehicles; includes *emissions generated by *fossil fuel or alternative fuel extraction, production, distribution, and *combustion. May be divided into stages of *well-to-tank and *tank-to-wheels emissions.

wetland

An area of land that is periodically saturated with water and characterized by vegetation adapted for life in saturated-soil conditions. *See also* bog; fen; marsh; palustrine wetland; swamp.

wetland delineation
The process of identifying the location and size of a *wetland for the purposes of meeting regulations.

wetland mitigation *See* mitigation, wetland.

white water
A term for the water that evaporates directly into the atmosphere without having been used productively; sometimes considered the nonproductive part of *green water.

wicked problems
Problems that are difficult or impossible to solve because they are complex, interconnected, and continually evolving.

wilderness
Historical term for *landscapes not impacted by humans.

wildlife
Nonhuman and nondomesticated animals.

wildlife overpass
A *corridor over a road serving as a crossing for animals which prevents their interaction with vehicles.

wildlife refuge
An area set aside for the protection of *wildlife where hunting and fishing are either prohibited or strictly controlled.

wind
The movement of air in the *atmosphere; a by-product of *solar radiation.

windbreak
A row of trees or other tall plants planted along the edges of farm fields to block *wind flow and protect *soil from *erosion. Also known as a shelterbelt.

wind energy
*Kinetic energy from air currents arising from uneven heating of the Earth's surface.

wind farm
A group of *wind turbines.

windmill
A device that uses mechanical power from *wind to operate low-speed machines such as water pumps.

wind power
*Power generated using a *wind turbine to convert the *mechanical energy of the wind into *electrical energy.

wind shear
A difference in *wind speed and direction between slightly different *elevations.

wind tower
An architectural element found in the Middle East that uses the *stack effect to cool interior spaces. Also known as a wind catcher. *See also* tower, wind turbine.

wind turbine
A machine consisting of blades and a generator that produces *electricity by converting *kinetic energy from *wind into *electrical energy.

wing wall
A small vertical projection on the outside of a building used to direct air flow. Also known as a fin wall.

wolf tree
A tree with a full crown and large branches that is evidence of having developed in the open, now surrounded by dissimilar upright, younger trees.

wood fuel

Any *energy source that comes from woody *biomass. *See also* biogas; cellulosic ethanol; charcoal; fuelwood; industrial fuelwood; wood pellets.

woodgas *See* synthesis gas.

wood pellet

A fuel for heating made from dried, compressed wood waste such as sawdust.

woonerf

A street with traffic calming measures and low speed limits designed to function as shared public space for pedestrians and cyclists.

work

The transfer of *energy; the *force exerted times the distance over which it is exerted.

worker-owned cooperative *See* cooperative.

World Bank

An international financial institution that provides grants and low-interest loans to developing countries with the stated goal of ending extreme *poverty and promoting shared prosperity.

worldview

A framework of assumptions and beliefs through which one sees and interprets the world.

worm castings

Nutrient-rich fecal matter excreted by earthworms.

XYZ

xenobiotic
A *synthetic *chemical substance which is foreign to living systems.

xeriscape
*Drought-tolerant landscaping designed to minimize the need for water.

zero energy *See* net zero energy.

zero waste
An approach in which every material is a *nutrient and *waste does not build up.

zoning
The regulatory practice of separating land areas by *land use type, with certain uses permitted and other uses prohibited within each zone.

zooplankton
Microscopic marine *consumers who live suspended in water and feed on *phytoplankton.

Bibliography

Agency for Toxic Substances and Disease Registry. *Glossary of Terms*. 2016. www.atsdr.cdc.gov/glossary.html

Ahmadi, Mehdi. *Environmental Engineering Dictionary*. 2016. www.ecologydictionary.org/Environmental-Engineering-Dictionary/

American Geological Institute (AGI). *Environmental Science: Understanding Our Changing Earth*. Clifton Park, New York: Delmar, 2011.

Apfelbaum, Steven I. and Alan W. Haney. *Restoring Ecological Health to Your Land*. Washington, DC: Island Press, 2010.

Barnett, Dianna Lopez and William D. Browning. *A Primer on Sustainable Building*, revised ed. Snowmass, CO: Rocky Mountain Institute, 2007.

Birkeland, Janis. *Design for Sustainability: A Sourcebook of Integrated Eco-logical Solutions*. London: Earthscan Publications, 2000.

Blaustein, Richard. "Predicting Tipping Points." *World Policy Journal* vol. 32 no. 1 (Spring 2015): 32–41.

Bradshaw, Vaughn. *The Building Environment: Active and Passive Control Systems*, 3rd ed. New York: John Wiley, 2006.

British Columbia Ministry of Education. *Sustainability Course Content: A Curriculum Framework*. Victoria: Ministry of Education, n.d.

Brown, G.Z. and Mark DeKay. *Sun, Wind & Light*, 2nd ed. New York: John Wiley, 2000.

Chen, Martha Alter. *The Informal Economy: Theories and Policies*. Cambridge, MA: WIEGO, 2012.

Christian, David. *Maps of Time: An Introduction to Big History*, 2nd ed. Berkeley, CA: University of California Press, 2011.

Clark, William C. "Sustainability Science: A Room of Its Own." *PNAS* vol. 104, no. 6 (Feb. 6, 2007): 1737–1738.

Cockrall-King, Jennifer. *Food and the City: Urban Agriculture and the New Food Revolution*. Amherst, New York: Prometheus Books, 2012.

Cox, J. Robert. *Environmental Communication and the Public Sphere*, 3rd ed. London: Sage Publications, 2012.

Cradle to Cradle Products Innovation Institute. *C2C Certified Product Standard*, Version 3.0. Charlottesville, VA: McDonough Braungart Design Chemistry, LLC, 2012. www.c2ccertified.org

Cunningham, William P. and Mary Ann Cunningham. *Environmental Science: A Global Concern*, 11th ed. New York: McGraw-Hill, 2010.

Curl, James Stevens. *Dictionary of Architecture*. Oxford, UK: Oxford University Press, 1999.

Czernik, Stefan. *Fundamentals of Charcoal Production*. Newcastle, UK: IBI Conference on Biochar, Sustainability and Security in a Changing Climate, 2008.

Daly, Herman E. and Joshua Farley. *Ecological Economics: Principles and Applications*. Washington, DC: Island Press, 2003.

Dramstad, Wenech E., James D. Olson, and Richard T.T. Forman. *Landscape Ecology Principles in Landscape Architecture and Land-Use Planning*. Washington, DC: Island Press, 1996.

Edwards, Andrés R. *The Sustainability Revolution: Portrait of a Paradigm Shift*. Gabriola Island, BC: New Society Publishers, 2005.

Edwards, Paul, ed. *The Encyclopedia of Philosophy*. New York: Macmillan, 1967.

EIA. *Energy Glossary*. n.d. www.eia.gov/tools/glossary/index.cfm

———. *Energy Efficiency Glossary*. n.d. www.eia.gov/emeu/efficiency/ee_gloss.htm

Ellen MacArthur Foundation. *The New Plastics Economy: Rethinking the Future of Plastics*. Cowes, UK: Ellen MacArthur Foundation, 2016.

———. *Towards the Circular Economy: Accelerating the Scale-up across Global Supply Chains*. Geneva, SW: World Economic Forum, 2014.

European Environment Agency (EEA). *Glossary*. n.d. http://glossary.eea.europa.eu//

Evans, J.P. *Environmental Governance*. London: Routledge, 2012.

Ewing, B., D. Moore, S. Goldfinger, A. Oursler, A. Reed, and M. Wackernagel. *The Ecological Footprint Atlas 2010*. Oakland, CA: Global Footprint Network, 2010.

Fiksel, Joseph. *Design for Environment*, 2nd ed. New York: McGraw-Hill, 2009.

Food and Agriculture Organization of the United Nations (FAO). www.fao.org/home/en/

France, Robert L. *Wetland Design: Principles and Practices for Landscape Architects and Land-Use Planners*. New York: W.W. Norton, 2002.

Frumkin, Howard. *Environmental Health: From Global to Local*, 2nd ed. San Francisco, CA: Jossey-Bass, 2010.

German Advisory Council on Global Change (WBGU). *World in Transition: A Social Contract for Sustainability*. Berlin: WBGU, 2011.

Gliessman, Stephen R., ed. *Agroecosystem Sustainability: Developing Practice Strategies*. Boca Raton, FL: CRC Press, 2000.

Global Footprint Network. *Glossary*. 2016. www.footprintnetwork.org/en/index.php/GFN/page/glossary/

Global Reporting Initiative (GRI). *G4 Sustainability Reporting Guidelines*. Amsterdam: Global Reporting Initiative, 2013.

Graedel, T.E. and B. R. Allenby. *Industrial Ecology*, 2nd ed. Upper Saddle River, NJ: Prentice Hall, 2003.

Green, Tracy. *Dictionary of Global Sustainability*. New York: McGraw-Hill, 2012.

GRID-Arendal. *Kick the Habit: A UN Guide to Climate Neutrality.* Nairobi: UNEP, 2008.

Hambrey, Michael and Jürg Alean. *Glaciers,* 2nd ed. Cambridge: Cambridge University Press, 2004.

Haselbach, Liv. *The Engineering Guide to LEED-New Construction: Sustainable Construction for Engineers,* 2nd ed. McGraw-Hill Education, 2010.

Hill, Marquita K. *Understanding Environmental Pollution,* 3rd ed. Cambridge, UK: Cambridge University Press, 2010.

Hobbs, Richard J. "Environmental Management and Restoration in a Changing Climate." Chapter 3 in Jelte van Andel and James Aronson, eds. *Restoration Ecology: The New Frontier,* 2nd ed. Chichester, UK: Wiley-Blackwell, 2012. 23–29.

Hobbs, Richard, Eric Higgs, and Carol Hall, eds. *Novel Ecosystems: Intervening in the New Ecological World Order.* Oxford, UK: Wiley-Blackwell, 2013.

Houghton, John. *Global Warming: The Complete Briefing,* 4th ed. Cambridge: Cambridge University Press, 2009.

Houtman, Anne, Susan Karr, and Jeneen Interlandi. *Environmental Science for a Changing World.* New York: W.H. Freeman and Scientific American, 2013.

Hughes, J. David. *Drill, Baby, Drill: Can Unconventional Fuels Usher in a New Era of Energy Abundance?* 2nd ed. Santa Rosa, CA: Post Carbon Institute, 2013.

International Energy Agency (IEA). *Glossary.* 2016. www.iea.org/about/glossary/

International Living Future Institute. *Living Building Challenge 3.0.* Seattle, WA: International Living Future Institute, 2014.

International Union for Conservation of Nature (IUCN). 2016. www.iucn.org/

International Work Group for Indigenous Affairs (IWGIA). 2016. www.iwgia.org

IPCC. *Special Report: Renewable Energy Sources and Climate Change Mitigation (SRREN).* Geneva: IPCC, 2012.

———. *Climate Change 2013: The Physical Science Basis. Contribution of Working Group I to the Fifth Assessment Report of the Intergovernmental Panel on Climate Change.* (Stocker, T. F., D. Qin, G.-K. Plattner, M. Tignor, S. K. Allen, J. Boschung, A. Nauels, Y. Xia, V. Bex, and P. M. Midgley, eds.). Cambridge, UK: Cambridge University Press, 2013.

———. *Climate Change 2014: Mitigation of Climate Change. Contribution of Working Group III to the Fifth Assessment Report of the Intergovernmental Panel on Climate Change.* (Edenhofer, O., R. Pichs-Madruga, Y. Sokona, E. Farahani, S. Kadner, K. Seyboth, A. Adler, I. Baum, S. Brunner, P. Eickemeier, B. Kriemann, J. Savolainen, S. Schlömer, C. von Stechow, T. Zwickel, and J. C. Minx, eds.). Cambridge, UK: Cambridge University Press, 2014.

Johnson, Bart R. and Kristina Hill, eds. *Ecology and Design: Frameworks for Learning.* Washington, DC: Island Press, 2002.

Johnston, David and Scott Gibson. *Green from the Ground Up: A Builder's Guide.* Newtown, CT: Taunton Press, 2008.

Jorgensen, Sven Erik and Brian D. Fath, eds. *Encyclopedia of Ecology.* Amsterdam: Elsevier Science, 2008.

Kates, Robert W. "What Kind of a Science Is Sustainability Science?" *Proceedings of the National Academy of Sciences* vol. 108 no. 49 (December 6, 2011): 19449–19450.

Keller, Edward A. and Daniel B. Botkin. *Essential Environmental Science*. New York: John Wiley, 2008.

Kibert, Charles J. *Sustainable Construction: Green Building Design and Delivery*, 3rd ed. New York: John Wiley, 2012.

Kopnina, Helen and Eleanor Shoreman-Ouimet, eds. *Sustainability: Key Issues*. London: Routledge, 2015.

Kump, Lee R., James F. Kasting, and Robert G. Crane. *The Earth System*, 3rd ed. Upper Saddle River, NJ: Prentice Hall, 2010.

Kwok, Alison G. and Walter T. Grondzik. *The Green Studio Handbook: Environmental Strategies for Schematic Design*. Oxford: Architectural Press, 2007.

LaGro, James A., Jr. *Site Analysis*, 2nd ed. New York: John Wiley, 2008.

Lechner, Norbert. *Heating, Cooling, Lighting: Sustainable Design Methods for Architects*, 3rd ed. New York: John Wiley, 2008.

Leppo, Holly Williams. *LEED Prep O&M: What You Really Need to Know to Pass the LEED AP Operations & Maintenance Exam*. Belmont, CA: Professional Publications (PPI), 2009.

Levin, Simon E., ed. *Encyclopedia of Biodiversity*, 2nd ed. Amsterdam: Academic Press, 2013.

Lovelock, James. *Gaia: A New Look at Life on Earth*. Oxford: Oxford University Press, 2000.

———. *The Revenge of Gaia*. New York: Basic Books, 2006.

Lovins, Amory B. *Reinventing Fire*. White River Junction, VT: Chelsea Green Publishing, 2011.

Maczulak, Anne. *Waste Treatment: Reducing Global Waste*. New York: Facts On File, 2010.

Mann, Michael E. and Lee R. Kump. *Dire Predictions: Understanding Global Warming – the Illustrated Guide to the Findings of the IPCC*. New York: DK Publishing, 2008.

Margulis, Lynn and Dorion Sagan. *What Is Life?* Berkeley, CA: University of California Press, 2000.

Marsh, William M. *Landscape Planning: Environmental Applications*, 5th ed. New York: John Wiley, 2010.

Meadows, Donella. *Thinking in Systems: A Primer*. White River, VT: Chelsea Green, 2008.

Mendler, Sandra, William Odell, and Mary Ann Lazarus. *The HOK Guidebook to Sustainable Design*, 2nd ed. New York: John Wiley, 2006.

Merchant, Carolyn. *American Environmental History: An Introduction*. New York: Columbia University Press, 2007.

Millennium Ecosystem Assessment. *Ecosystems and Human Well-Being: Synthesis*. Washington, DC: Island Press, 2005.

Miller, G. Tyler, Jr., and Scott E. Spoolman. *Living in the Environment: Concepts, Connections, and Solutions*, 16th ed. Belmont, CA: Brooks/Cole, 2009.

Mitsch, William J. and James G. Gosselink. *Wetlands*, 4th ed. New York: John Wiley, 2007.

Moore, Robin C. and Allen Cooper. *Nature Play & Learning Places: Creating and Managing Places Where Children Engage with Nature*. Raleigh, NC: Natural Learning Initiative and Reston, VA: National Wildlife Federation, 2014.

Morse, Roger and Don Acker. *Indoor Air Quality: Whole Building Design Guide*. Washington, DC: National Institute of Building Sciences, 2009. www.wbdg.org/resources/env_iaq.php.

Munier, Nolberto. *Introduction to Sustainability: Road to a Better Future*. Dordrecht, The Netherlands: Springer, 2005.

National Institute of Building Sciences. *A Common Definition for Zero Energy Buildings*. Washington, DC: US Department of Energy (DOE) Energy Efficiency and Renewable Energy (EERE), 2015.

Natural Resources Conservation Service (NRDC). *Stream Corridor Restoration: Principles, Processes, and Practices*. Washington, DC: Natural Resources Conservation Service, 1998.

Newman, Peter and Isabella Jennings. *Cities as Sustainable Ecosystems: Principles and Practices*. Washington, DC: Island Press, 2008.

OECD. *Glossary of Statistical Terms*. 2007. https://stats.oecd.org/glossary

OSU Extension Service. *Watershed Stewardship: A Learning Guide*. Corvallis, OR: Oregon State University, 2005.

Page, Scott E. *Understanding Complexity*. Chantilly, VA: The Teaching Company, 2009.

Pahl, Greg. *Power from the People: How to Organize, Finance, and Launch Local Energy Projects*. White River Junction, VT: Chelsea Green Publishing, 2012.

Park, Chris and Michael Allaby, eds. *A Dictionary of Environment and Conservation*, 2nd ed. Oxford, UK: Oxford University Press, 2013.

Pepper, Ian L., Charles P. Gerba, and Mark L. Brusseau, eds. *Environmental and Pollution Science*, 2nd ed. Boston: Academic Press, 2006.

Perlman, Dan L. and Jeffrey C. Milder. *Practical Ecology for Planners, Developers, and Citizens*. Washington, DC: Island Press, 2004.

Platt, Brenda, David Ciplet, Kate M. Bailey, and Eric Lombardi. *Stop Trashing the Climate*. Washington, DC: Institute for Local Self-Reliance, 2008.

Presidio Graduate School. *Dictionary of Sustainable Management*. 2017. www.sustainabilitydictionary.com

Primack, Richard B. *A Primer of Conservation Biology*, 4th ed. Sunderland, MA: Sinauer Associates, 2008.

Reynolds, John S. *Courtyards: Aesthetic, Social, and Thermal Delight*. New York: John Wiley, 2001.

Riley, Ann L. *Restoring Streams in Cities*. Washington, DC: Island Press, 1998.

Simonsen, Sturle Hauge. *Resilience Dictionary*. 2016. Stockholm Resilience Centre, 2007. www.stockholmresilience.su.se

Spirn, Anne Whiston. *The Language of Landscape*. New Haven, CT: Yale University Press, 1998.

Steiner, Frederick. *The Living Landscape: An Ecological Approach to Landscape Planning*, 2nd ed. New York: McGraw-Hill, 1999.

Stevens, E.E. *Green Plastics: An Introduction to the New Science of Biodegradable Plastics*. Princeton, NJ: Princeton University Press, 2002.

Stockholm Resilience Centre. *Applying Resilience Thinking: Seven Principles for Building Resilience in Social-Ecological Systems*. Stockholm, Sweden: Stockholm Resilience Centre, 2015.

————. *What Is Resilience? An Introduction to Social-Ecological Research*. Stockholm, SW: Stockholm Resilience Centre, 2015.

Strom, Steven, Kurt Nathan, and Jake Woland. *Site Engineering for Landscape Architects*, 6th ed. New York: John Wiley, 2012.

Sullivan, Chip. *Garden and Climate*. New York: McGraw-Hill, 2002.

Sustainability Consortium. *Glossary*. 2016. www.sustainabilityconsortium.org/glossary/

Sustainable Scale. 2003. www.sustainablescale.org

Taleb, Nassim Nicholas. *The Black Swan: The Impact of the Highly Improbable*, 2nd ed. New York: Random House, 2010.

TEEB. *The Economics of Ecosystems and Biodiversity: Mainstreaming the Economics of Nature: A Synthesis of the Approach, Conclusions and Recommendations of TEEB*, 2010.

Thumann, Albert, Terry Niehus, and William J. Younger. *Handbook of Energy Audits*, 9th ed. Lilburn, GA: Fairmont Press, 2012.

Toensmeier, Eric. *The Carbon Farming Solution*. White River Junction, VT: Chelsea Green, 2016.

Transportation Research Board. *Urban Public Transportation Glossary*. Washington, DC: Transportation Research Board, 1989.

Trefil, James and Robert Hazen. *The Sciences: An Integrated Approach*, 6th ed. New York: John Wiley, 2010.

UNEP. *Communicating Sustainability: How to Produce Effective Public Campaigns*. Nairobi, Kenya: United Nations Environment Programme, 2005.

————. *Vital GeoGraphics*. Nairobi, Kenya: United Nations Environment Programme, 2009.

Union of Concerned Scientists. *The Root of the Problem: What's Driving Tropical Deforestation Today?* Cambridge, MA: Union of Concerned Scientists, 2011.

United Nations. *Water in a Changing World: United Nations World Water Development Report*, 3rd ed. Paris: UNESCO, 2009.

University of Oregon Campus Zero Waste Program. *Zero Waste Campus Toolkit*. Eugene, OR: University of Oregon and College and University Recycling Coalition, 2014.

US Department of Energy, Energy Information Administration (EIA). *Glossary*. 2016. www.eia.doe.gov/

US Department of the Interior. *Best Management Practices for Reducing Visual Impacts of Renewable Energy Facilities on BLM-Administered Lands*. Cheyenne, WY: Bureau of Land Management, 2013.

US Department of Labor, Bureau of Labor Statistics. 2016. www.bls.gov

US Department of Transportation (DOT), Transportation and Climate Change Clearinghouse. *Glossary*. 2016. http://climate.dot.gov/glossary.html

US EPA. *Air Quality Glossary*. 2013. www.epa.gov/airquality/community/glossary.html

————. *Clean Energy Glossary*. 2016. www.epa.gov/cleanenergy/energy-and-you/glossary.html

————. *Climate Change Glossary*. 2016. www.epa.gov/climatechange/glossary.html

———. *Decision Maker's Guide to Solid Waste Management*, Volume II. EPA Office of Solid Waste and Emergency Response, 1995.

———. *Drinking Water Glossary*. Washington, DC: EPA, 2004.

———. *Green Power Glossary*. 2016. www.epa.gov/greenpower/pubs/glossary.htm

———. *Green Products Glossary*. 2016. www.epa.gov/greenproducts/glossary/

———. *Greening the EPA Glossary*. 2016. www.epa.gov/greeningepa/glossary.htm

———. *Heat Island Glossary*. 2013. www.epa.gov/heatisld/resources/glossary.htm

———. *Indoor Air Quality Glossary*. 2013. www.epa.gov/iaq/glossary.html

———. *Life Cycle Assessment: Principles and Practice*. Cincinnati, OH: National Risk Management Research Laboratory, 2006.

———. *Measuring Recycling: A Guide for State and Local Governments*. Washington, DC: EPA, 1997.

———. *National Pollutant Discharge Elimination System (NPDES) Glossary*. 2013. http://cfpub.epa.gov/npdes/glossary.cfm?program_id=0

———. *Ozone Layer Protection Glossary*. 2016. www.epa.gov/ozone/defns.html

———. *Paper Recycling Glossary*. 2013. www.epa.gov/wastes/conserve/materials/paper/resources/glossary.htm

———. *Protecting and Restoring America's Watersheds*. Washington, DC: EPA Office of Water, 2001.

———. *Purchasing Glossary*. 2013. www.epa.gov/epp/pubs/cleaners/concepts.htm

———. *Report on the Environment Glossary*. 2016. www.epa.gov/ncea/roe/glossary.htm

———. *Resource Conservation and Recovery Act Glossary*. Washington, DC: National Center for Environmental Assessment (NCEA), 2015.

———. *Superfund Glossary*. 2013. www.epa.gov/superfund/programs/reforms/glossary.htm

———. *Sustainable Manufacturing Glossary*. 2016. www.epa.gov/sustainablemanufacturing/glossary.htm

———. *Water Educator Glossary*. 2016. http://water.epa.gov/learn/resources/glossary.cfm

———. *What Is Integrated Solid Waste Management?* EPA Office of Solid Waste and Emergency Response, 2002. www.epa.gov/wastes/wycd/catbook/you.htm

USGBC. *Green Building and LEED Core Concepts*, 2nd ed. Upper Saddle River, NJ: Prentice Hall, 2011.

US Global Change Research Program (USGCRP). *Climate Change, Wildlife and Wildlands: A Toolkit for Formal and Informal Educators*. USGCRP, 2009. www.globalchange.gov/climate-toolkit

Vesilind, P. Aarne, Susan M. Morgan, and Lauren G. Heine. *Introduction to Environmental Engineering*. Stamford, CT: Cengage Learning, 2004.

Vries, Bert J.M. de. *Sustainability Science*. New York: Cambridge University Press, 2013.

Wackernagel, Mathis and William Rees. *Our Ecological Footprint: Reducing Human Impact on the Earth*. Gabriola Island, BC: New Society Publishers, 1995.

Walker, Brian and David Salt. *Resilience Practice*. Washington, DC: Island Press, 2012.

Wessels, Tom. *The Myth of Progress: Toward a Sustainable Future*. Burlington, VT: University of Vermont Press, 2006.

Wheeler, Benjamin, Gilda Wheeler, and Wendy Church. *It's All Connected: A Comprehensive Guide to Global Issues and Sustainable Solutions*. Seattle, WA: Facing the Future: People and the Planet, 2005.

Wijkman, Anders and Johan Rockström. *Bankrupting Nature: Denying Our Planetary Boundaries*. London: Routledge, 2012.

Wolfe, David W. *Tales from the Underground: A Natural History of Subterranean Life*. New York: Basic Books, 2001.

Wolfson, Richard. *Earth's Changing Climate*. Chantilly, VA: The Teaching Company, 2007.

———. *Energy, Environment, and Climate*. New York: W.W. Norton, 2008.

Yeang, Ken. *EcoDesign: A Manual for Ecological Design*. London: Wiley-Academy, 2006.